# SUNSHOWER

# SUNSHOWER

## Karen Kenyon

Richard Marek Publishers
New York

The author gratefully acknowledges the following for permission to reprint previously published material:

Elsevier-Dutton Publishing Co., Inc., for one line from "There Are Men Too Gentle to Live Among Wolves," excerpted from *There Are Men Too Gentle to Live Among Wolves* by James Kavanaugh, copyright © 1970 by James Kavanaugh.

Fox Fanfare Music, Inc., for a portion of "The Rose" by Amanda McBroom, © 1977 and 1979 by Fox Fanfare Music, Inc. All Rights Reserved.

Harcourt Brace Jovanovich, Inc., for a portion of "Little Giddings" from *Four Quartets* by T. S. Eliot, copyright 1943 by T. S. Eliot; renewed 1971 by Esme Valerie Eliot, and for lines from "love is the every only god," excerpted from *Complete Poems 1913–1962* by e. e. cummings, copyright 1940 by e. e. cummings, copyright renewed © 1968 by Marion Morehouse Cummings.

Harper & Row, Publishers, Inc., for a poem by Edna St. Vincent Millay from *Collected Poems*, copyright 1921, 1948, by Edna St. Vincent Millay.

Little, Brown and Company for a line from *The Magus: A Revised Version* by John Fowles, copyright 1978 by John Fowles.

New Directions Publishing Company for "And Death Shall Have No Dominion" from *The Poems of Dylan Thomas*, copyright 1943 by New Directions Publishing Corporation.

New Directions Publishing Corporation and the Estate of Stevie Smith for "Not Waving but Drowning" from *Selected Poems* by Stevie Smith, copyright 1964 by Stevie Smith.

W. W. Norton & Co., Inc., for a line from *Letters to a Young Poet*, by Rainer Maria Rilke, translation by M. D. Herter Norton, copyright 1934 by W. W. Norton & Co., Inc., copyright renewed 1962 by M. D. Herter Norton.

Charles Scribner's Sons, a division of the Scribner Book Companies, Inc., for Edwin Arlington Robinson's poem, "Richard Cory," from *The Children of the Night*.

Seabury Press, Inc., for a portion of C. S. Lewis's *A Grief Observed*, copyright 1961 by N. W. Clerk.

Warner Bros. Music for lyrics from "Hotel California" by Don Felder, Don Henley and Glenn Frey, © 1976 by Red Cloud Music, Cass Country Music & Fingers Music. All Rights Reserved.

Library of Congress Cataloging in Publication Data

Kenyon, Karen.
  Sunshower.

  1. Widows—United States. 2. Suicide—United States.
3. Widows—United States—Conduct of life. I. Title.
HQ1058.5.U5K45      362.8′3      81-3718
ISBN 0-399-90130-2              AACR2

Thanks go to my family and friends, those mentioned in the book and those others known in my heart who gave me hope, encouragement, and love, as I came through this passage; and I want to thank a special friend, Paul Brenner, M.D., for his support, love, and insight. I also wish to thank Judy Gingold, Editor of "My Turn" at *Newsweek,* for publishing "A Survivor's Notes" (April 30, 1979); the many kind people who wrote to me after "A Survivor's Notes" appeared, portions of whose letters I gratefully acknowledge quoting here; Jane Jordan Browne, my agent, for her encouragement and confidence; and Richard Marek, my publisher, for giving tangible life to these thoughts.

This book is dedicated to the memory of Dick, and the life he had in him, but most especially it is dedicated to Richard, our son, and all the life he has ahead of him.

*Richard Cory*

Whenever Richard Cory went down town,
  We people on the pavement looked at him:
He was a gentleman from sole to crown,
  Clean favored, and imperially slim.

And he was always quietly arrayed,
  And he was always human when he talked;
But still he fluttered pulses when he said,
  "Good-morning," and he glittered when he walked.

And he was rich,—yes, richer than a king,—
  And admirably schooled in every grace:
In fine, we thought that he was everything
  To make us wish that we were in his place.

So on we worked, and waited for the light,
  And went without the meat, and cursed the bread;
And Richard Cory, one calm summer night,
  Went home and put a bullet through his head.

                    Edwin Arlington Robinson

*Not Waving But Drowning*

Nobody heard him, the dead man,
But still he lay moaning:
I was much further out than you thought
And not waving but drowning.

Poor chap, he always loved larking
And now he's dead
It must have been too cold for him his heart gave way,
They said.

Oh, no no no, it was too cold always
(Still the dead one lay moaning)
I was much too far out all my life
And not waving but drowning.

Stevie Smith

One night my brother and his wife took their little girl, Caitlin, who was three, outside to look at the stars.

Caitlin said, "If I had butterfly wings, I would fly to those stars."

Marcia, her mother, wanting to give her reality, said, "But honey, birds and butterflies can fly, but people can't."

Caitlin replied, "Well, maybe I could go to the dump and find an old pair of wings."

# Contents

# Prelude

Much is written about "causes" and "prevention" of suicide, but little is said about the shock, the sorrow, the shame, sense of failure, and guilt most survivors feel, and little is said about how life goes on afterwards. More and more families and friends are left as survivors each day.

When someone takes his or her own life, it is seen as the saddest statement anyone could ever make. At least in our culture, this is so. Suicide is covered up, hidden by family and friends. It is seen as a mark on the lives of those connected with it. But it happens. It is part of our human experience.

*Sunshower* is about light that comes after darkness, and it is about the light that is, even in darkness. It is about those sunshowers that are our release and baptism into more life.

This book is an outgrowth of an essay I wrote for *Newsweek* ("My Turn," April 30, 1979, "A Survivor's Notes"), dealing with my husband's suicide, and with the questions and choices left to me, my son, and all others in our situation.

My husband, Dick, and I had been married almost sixteen years, and for the three before that we had been inseparable.

17

We had a wonderful son, Richard, who was twelve when his father died. We had had a baby girl named Johanna, who was a Down's Syndrome child and lived six months. Dick worked for the University of California in an administrative position. I did a little freelance writing and some art work. We owned a house in a fairly comfortable neighborhood. We had friends. We had no major problems, no illnesses, no great debts.

One night, instead of coming home as he always did, Dick left a suicide note in his car, then he must have walked around all night. At daybreak, as the sun rose, he jumped to his death from an eleven-story building on the campus where he worked.

All dreams stopped. All reality was undone. The mirror of life was shattered.

There were no observable clues, no threats of destruction, just a slightly noticeable withdrawal.

He was a man who seemed to have so much—thirty-eight years old, attractive, intelligent. He was an extremely sensitive, logical, and gentle man. It always seemed he had so much to give, but how much did he ultimately give to himself? Did he throw himself away like a piece of crumpled paper, or did he give himself in a final offering to life? Maybe the answer lies somewhere in between.

Outwardly, he led a full, happy life. Inwardly he must have felt terribly thwarted, pressured. Perhaps he felt grief, perhaps he felt despair.

His note to me began, "Karen, This job has killed me."

Had his job, which did not not suit him, but which he continually tried to rise above, finally swallowed the last remnant of spirit in him?

If he had been able to somehow fight back—take the risk of "dropping out," of killing the job—would he have had to kill himself?

If he had been able to voice his pain and frustration, and to believe he could find a listening ear, could he have been saved?

If those of us who knew him closely had seen him, really seen him, and not just our illusions of him, could he have lived?

*Sunshower* is not the story of why he did it, because there are

18

no real answers, only real questions. It tells of living beyond loss and shock, beyond a world turned inside out. This is not a book about death. It tells the story of coming back from the valley of dying, of letting go and making a choice for living.

I write this book for everyone, for we all tread a line between life and non-life everyday—life is fragile, love is fragile—and I write it for those who have had to grapple with devastating mysteries, who have had to find their way in the void, who have had to find a light switch in the darkest of rooms.

Maybe that light won't be found as soon as we would wish, or come all at once, and maybe many steps will have to be taken, one by one, in order to reach it, but we, the survivors, do have a common goal—to work toward a release into life, just as our mate, parent, child, or friend worked toward a release into death. By facing what has happened, not denying it or our feelings, and then going on, ironically the event can push us into life deeply and transform us. Each day we live, we are choosing life, creating life. That is the essence of this book. The word, "sunshower," seems to crystallize something very essential to me—the union of sadness and joy, of dark and light—the point where we live.

It is just my story, not a story with answers. It is a mystery story in the sense that life is a mystery. It is one person's story, but I feel that all our struggles and all our joys are somehow one.

We all suffer when we lose someone we love. Those we love are extensions of ourselves, and so when they die, we feel that part of us dies too. That is hard enough, but when that death was chosen, then as survivors we are terribly wounded. In our struggle to understand, we also have to cut ourselves free from the act itself—not from the person, or our love for him or her—and we have to realize that each person is ultimately responsible for his or her own destiny. And I believe we have to learn and grow beyond the pain—go on from such an act, even nurture ourselves with it. That is the creative act.

This is the story, pressed through the screen of my memory and emotions, of Dick's and my life together, and it is the story of the aftermath—the survival and recovery of my son and me.

This is a story of loss, but it is also a story of rebirth.

19

# Prologue

When I was five or six I was tap dancing with two other little girls on the stage at Central Grade School in Guthrie, Oklahoma. Everything was going fine—piano tinkling, our taps sounding on the hardwood floor, curls bobbing, small painted lips smiling, our green and red dresses bouncing—when suddenly without warning I fell flat on my face. In an instant I was up, catching the dance step again, secretly hoping I had popped back so fast no one would notice. The crowd clapped and cheered. This was surprising and strange to me, and I knew then, of course, that they had noticed.

Later my mother told me she was amazed. She expected me to run off the stage crying. But I just wanted to keep dancing. The music hadn't stopped, and I didn't want to either.

K. Kenyon

# SKY

I am afraid
you will know
me
and no longer see
your vision of me,

so
I will try
to run ahead
away from a hell or heaven
I can't enter.

I move in sleep
and roll close to you
seeking my own fantasy,
and I awaken to the sound of rain.

(November, 1974)

23

# 1 / Our Life—The First Beginning

Memory, illusion, dream—it all exists only in my mind now. The circle of our life is complete. I pull out fragments, scenes, and scattered pictures—a mosaic of days . . .

I first met Dick at a Roaring Twenties party. It was 1959, at the University of New Mexico, in Albuquerque. It was instant "like," if not yet love. He wore a derby on his thick dark hair, a fake mustache, a red vest, and a garter on one arm. He was slim and tall, and every now and then his soft green eyes caught mine. His manner was unaffected, his movements nonchalant. He was nineteen, and I was twenty.

The several strands of long beads I wore with my green fringed dress clanked and swung around as we danced.

"God, you're really too much with all that stuff around your neck," he teased. It was the kind of playful insult that sometimes comes with long-term friendship, and this endeared him to me, caused me to feel close to him. At the same time the teasing seemed to mask a certain shyness, I thought. I recognized it. It was in me too.

I recall being drawn to Dick, and felt that if he cared for me,

25

I wouldn't say no to him, that this was it. The feeling was so strong it almost frightened me. Intimacy was there from the start. I felt a sense of knowing Dick that went beyond words.

At the same time I sensed what felt to me like a small dark cloud over his head. It was as if there was a little lost boy in Dick. He had a trace of cynicism about him that he tried to cover with the humor—something skeptical—something almost disillusioned about him. I remember being touched by this aspect of his personality and feeling that the skepticism must come from his wanting to believe so much.

This cloud seemed small though, mixed in with the light of his intelligence, his sensitivity, the teasing, and the fun.

I soon forgot the touch of darkness, the deep sense of vulnerability I sensed in him, and didn't think of that particular image of a cloud again until everything was over. I pushed it away, and saw him in some ways as he was, and in some ways as I wanted to see him.

I believe I was attracted to him initially because his wit lifted me and gave me a feeling of happiness, and of closeness to him; and I fell in love with him because his personality was riding gently on top of enormous sensitivity—so strong you could almost touch it, so quivering it stuck out all over him— and because he *cared*—about other people, about events, about what had happened, about what was happening, and about what was going to happen. I fell in love with him because he was so alive, because when he looked at me, or anyone, you could almost see inside him. He was not outwardly revealing, in fact he seemed to avoid that, but it was possible to catch glimpses. These glimpses he gave of himself were fleeting, and yet there was no real veil of pretense, no hostility guarding the gate of his soul, just a guarded hesitancy. And there was a look of almost innocence about him, that he himself was innocent of.

A few weeks after we met, a friend called to tell me Dick was in the hospital. He'd had an emergency appendectomy. I went to the hospital to visit him. Another girlfriend of his was walking down the hall from the room as I approached. My heart began to beat faster. I began to think I shouldn't have come.

26

Dick was a little groggy from the medication, but seemed glad to see me. He also was feeling very annoyed at the way one nurse had been treating him—in a condescending, almost motherly way.

He asked me to pull the curtain all around his bed so that we could have privacy.

The next day I came back, and soon after I came in he told me to open the bedside table. When I did, I saw that his fraternity pin was in there—carefully placed.

"It's for you," he said. "If you want it."

Then, even though the curtain was once again drawn, we must have steamed up all the windows on that floor.

From then on, we were inseparable. We spent as much time together as possible, in between studying and part-time jobs.

We seldom disagreed. In fact the only quarrel I can recall during those days took place one evening on the sidewalk of the campus. Dick had thrown away several greeting cards I had made by hand and given him. In his "house cleaning" he hadn't chosen to keep them. I suppose my feelings were hurt, and I wanted some indication that the cards and I meant something to him, thinking somehow those cards stood for love. It was a quiet snow-fallen evening. Dick was anxious to end the discussion, to go to a class or a meeting, and so he walked away before anything was resolved.

I went to the library to wait for him. The quarrel or disagreement wasn't finished, and now was held in limbo for the two or so intervening hours. I remember worrying as I waited, thinking fearfully, "this is the end." He'd never just walked away, never left anything emotional unfinished before.

Time passed, and in a couple of hours I looked up from my books. Dick was standing there with a serious look on his face. "Let's go," he said. We talked, and I know I felt reassured, though I don't recall now what he said. The fact he came back was everything, and the fact he was so decisive with me meant a lot. It was, I think, the only time, in all the years I was with him, that I ever doubted what we had—that I ever doubted he would come back, or feared he wouldn't be around. I always felt so totally he was there that it never occurred to me he might someday be gone.

27

Several times during our college years he surprised me with bouquets of roses—not just one or two but a dozen—and each time a card would be included with words of love and of his own happiness, in small, cramped handwriting.

Because Dick was in Naval ROTC he was required not to marry until he graduated and received his commission in the Marine Corps. He complied, wanting what he felt was best for us in the long run. It seemed important to him to follow through with what he had planned and what seemed right. One of his fraternity brothers, also in NROTC, had been secretly married for a year, and I often wished, romantically, that Dick could be so daring—that we could take that risk. I often felt he was stubborn, and I knew he was immovable once he really made up his mind about something.

Three years passed, and on a crisp, bright day, Valentine's Day, 1963, the snow glistening on distant mountains in the mid-winter sun, we were married. Dick wore his uniform. Two days earlier he had been commissioned a second lieutenant in the Marine Corps. Now the four-year ROTC scholarship to UNM was to be paid back by spending four years in the Marine Corps. Dick had sought independence from his parents by taking that scholarship. For the next four years he would have to fulfill a role that always seemed incongruous.

I wore a white dress, a veil of French lace. My mother was there, trying to show happiness, but her eyes held that blend of joy and sadness mothers often feel at the weddings of their children. I was her only daughter, and we had been close. Now I was leaving—moving across the United States. Dick's parents and his family came from Illinois. My brother gave me away.

It was the beginning of what we expected to be a happy life. I felt that whatever happiness was—it lay on the other side of those vows. I felt everything was ahead of us. One of our favorite songs had been "Somewhere," from *West Side Story.* We were always waiting for that "place for us."

As soon as the ceremony was over and we walked down the aisle, tears came to me—of nervousness and happiness. Now we were "one." Now it was "until death do us part," but who ever listens to that line?

Going back is not to solve a mystery, or to find a cause. Perhaps going back is to see the gift that was there, and to retrace the steps that lead to today.

Our honeymoon was our drive from Albuquerque to Quantico, Virginia. We spent most of our first married year there while Dick was in basic training, learning to be a "Marine." I adjusted my life and learned how to be a "wife"—how to spend my days, how to clean my house—a very different life from my busy, active one before, involving work, school, my family, friends, and Dick.

We were close and playful the way newlyweds can be. I spent a lot of time during the day thinking up interesting dinners, and hours cleaning the house, trying to do everything right. We always had candles on the table. We went to plays, movies, and the National Gallery, in Washington, D.C. We played tennis, and when I didn't play well, which was usual, Dick would encourage me, challenge me to do better. We found a little puppy and brought her home, filled the house with plants, and lived the good life of a young officer and his wife. It seemed we really belonged together. We were a match. We bounced off each other well, and we came together well. At night we always slept with our arms around each other, and my head lay always on his shoulder. Our favorite song was "My Funny Valentine."

Dick never found fault with me—never complained about food, the house, or me personally. In fact he was never demanding of me. Sometimes I would become a bit angry at him—perhaps because of his occasional stubbornness, or perhaps because he had a certain passivity about him, and sometimes I wanted more interaction. I suppose on some level I felt I couldn't reach him. But even if I became upset, he never responded to me outwardly in an angry way. Sometimes he would pace around, but a quarrel seldom, if ever, occurred. Those times of even slight disagreement were rare. For the most part there was much compatibility. We had a real sense of belonging together.

We were in totally new surroundings. It was an exciting time to be around Washington. The Kennedys were in the White House, and their aura seemed to permeate the air.

It was also a time of contrasts—the black freedom march in Washington was held. Our new marriage was born in these times of beginning changes for everyone. And yet as I look back I sense a glossiness to those early days, as if we lived the fantasy we expected, as if we had somehow found "home" and now nothing could harm us or stand in our way.

Soon we both began to want a baby—to complete us, I thought, and myself, to fill us out as a family—but a pregnancy did not soon occur, as we both hoped and anticipated it would.

The days at Quantico were in general a blend of the days of training and the days off, which Dick always wanted to take advantage of. We'd drive to Washington or to historical sites nearby, and Dick's insatiable curiosity would devour all the information he could find. When in Washington he would drive all over, find obscure places I would never have been able to find. He never wasted a day or a chance to do or see something interesting. He always seemed to know all about and have a great interest in the outside world.

During the actual training, Dick never dropped out. He could endure. On the long marches and on the obstacle course, others would fall away, but Dick seemed to have the ability to set his mind and not give in to physical pain. During those days he would often come home looking tired beyond belief, as if his very soul were covered with the grime of playing war.

If I said, "It must have been awful," he'd say, "No sweat, Karen. You should have seen me!" He always felt proud if he could make it through something difficult. He expected much from himself, had a strong competitive streak, and seemed to constantly measure himself against some demanding inner standard.

Months after it began, in the late fall, basic training was over. Dick had made it through with high marks. Then orders came that he be stationed near Oceanside, California, at Camp Pendleton. As we drove back across the autumn countryside, we stopped at military "guest houses." They always had twin beds, but we always just slept in one. There is a closeness born of military life. You are together in what is often a strange world, and friendships with others are not deep because of the mobility.

One evening, a day or two into our drive, somewhere in the South, we stopped in a filling station. It was November, 1963. A small TV was turned on. The attendants were gathered around. We heard something about the President being dead. We thought, of course, that one of the older ex-Presidents had died—Truman or Eisenhower. Back in the car, turning on our radio, we learned the truth.

Once in California we settled near Camp Pendleton, in Oceanside—spent hours at the beach. We loved the ocean, and most weekends we took trips to the southern California sites. We felt fairly free. We had fun. There were few responsibilities. At least that is the way it seemed to me. I knew little of what went on with Dick each day at the base. He didn't speak much about his work.

A year later I conceived. Dick was sent for training in the Sierra Madre Mountains, in Mono County in northern California, for a few months. I was working, but we wanted to be together, and so I went with him. It seemed an ideal way to spend the summer. We stayed in a little fishing cabin in a beautiful tiny community that looked like postcards I had seen of Switzerland. But a month or so after arriving I began to have difficulty with the pregnancy, and at five months, we lost that baby in miscarriage. It was an incredible sadness for me, and for Dick too. Somehow we had never expected anything to go wrong. We had had a feeling of invulnerability. Once it was over we never knew what had caused it. There was anxiety now, about having children, and guilt, about reasons why. I began to see that things would not just work out well automatically as I had expected, that our finding one another didn't insure that our desires would be granted and life would unfold exactly as we wished. I realized events could happen over which we had no control.

Once back in San Diego I took long walks by the ocean. Only the power, force, and constancy of the waves could soothe me, or still the anxiety I felt. Dick was kind, supportive. His

31

strength was present, and yet his own disappointment and emotions were never much discussed. When pain or distress came along, it always seemed to be mine, and it seemed Dick could somehow handle everything. He could keep life stable, could give hope and encouragement.

Dick's career continued to grow in the Marine Corps. As soon as the required time passed, his rating was changed to first lieutenant. Now he had more responsibility. Now his role was even more clearly defined. But he needed some outlet, some form of self-expression. One day he made a metal sculpture in the base's welding shop. We went to the ceramics shop, and he spent hours painting some decanters he molded there. He carried around a paperback copy of *Naked Came I,* the biographical novel about Auguste Rodin, the sculptor, and read it during his breaks.

A year passed and for a few nights Dick didn't come home from work until the early hours of the morning. One night I asked him, "What's going on?" His company, he said, had to load ship for Vietnam. Without a warning they would all be gone in a matter of days. I felt fearful. This was so sudden. And I also had a strong suspicion I was again pregnant, though I had said nothing about it.

I was panicked. I had to fight my own war now. I was afraid of Dick's leaving, and afraid of losing this baby, too. I told him I wanted to talk to the Red Cross to see if anything could be done. He agreed. When I talked to the workers there they said I had a case, but that it was too late for intervention through them. All I could do, they said, was go straight to the colonel. This wasn't easy for a lieutenant's wife. In the colonel's office I poured out my story. He listened, and when I finished, he just sat there. Then he picked up the phone, asked for "Kenyon" to be sent to him; and later that day, after he had talked to Dick, the orders were changed.

Someone else went in Dick's place. I wonder now if that someone is alive today. And I wonder how different Dick's life would have been if he had gone. Would he have died then? Would he have been wounded, and how would that have changed his life? Would he have built more of a protective shell around himself to live in, and would that have been Dick?

32

Most of all though, would it have satisfied his craving to do his duty? He must have felt a tremendous conflict between duty to us as a family, and duty to whatever then was his job, and to country. When I think back I can almost remember seeing the turmoil in his eyes, but at the time I didn't want to see that. This sense of duty, of rightness, was always strong in Dick—a product of his Catholic upbringing, perhaps, of wanting to please? Or of being rewarded for achieving, and not for failing, as men always are in our society, as little boys always are? I don't know how it started, but I know he had it in him.

On one level, it was easy for us both to justify Dick's staying with me, easy to not want to go to a war which initially had no meaning, and which, it became increasingly apparent to us, we didn't believe in.

It was a time for people to test their beliefs, and there were stirrings everywhere. The Watts riot raged one hundred miles up the coast from us. Everyone was jarred to think—What do we really care about?

Dick never hesitated to make stands for issues or people he believed in. In fact I think it was an important part of him. Shortly after he was allowed to stay, a Marine sergeant and his wife who lived in our apartment building invited a black sergeant, ready to leave for Vietnam, to have dinner with them. The landlord was incensed that a black man would be in one of his apartments. He told the black sergeant to leave, told our friends they must move. The minute Dick heard about it he said we would move too. Within days he found us a place, packed and moved everything. I was having trouble with the pregnancy, and so couldn't even help. He did it totally on his own. He cared, and the inconvenience mattered nothing to him. Making a stand did.

Eight months later, after several miscarriage scares, Richard Laurence Kenyon persisted and was born—strapping and healthy. It was the happiest, highest moment of my life, and I believe of Dick's too. I'll never forget seeing, in the overhead mirror, the crowning of Richard. I could hardly believe that baby was really in me, and was really being born. This was before fathers were allowed in the delivery room, but I could

33

talk to Dick soon after, via the "blue" phone next to the delivery table. Later when I had Richard with me in my room, I looked at him and those baby-blue eyes looked right at me and made contact.

Dick was a proud and very happy father. How awkwardly he held Richard for the first time! As if he wanted to be so careful, as if he held a precious, delicate glass doll. And teasing! "Where had he come from?" Dick asked, "this baby with the reddish hair and robust physique!"

But the love and tenderness were evident in his face when he held his son on his lap and looked into his face.

Those were happy days, in our small apartment in Oceanside. I recall so clearly Dick coming home every night to play with his little "son-o" as he playfully called him, and the three of us going for walks on the pier in the pink-and-gold evenings.

Only one dark cloud hovered for a while on our newfound bliss. We had our first glimpse of loss. I was sitting on the couch one evening, feeding our month-old baby, when the phone rang. It was my grandmother. "Honey," she began, "your father has died." I recalled just sending him a photograph of Richard, his first grandchild. I wondered now if my dad had ever seen that picture. I felt some emotion, but the feeling of loss was not great. I had really lost him at age thirteen when my parents were divorced and my mother and brother and I had moved from Oklahoma to California. I had seen him only infrequently since then, yet when I was old enough he had made sure I went to college. He had cared about me in his way, but in so many ways I didn't feel I knew him. Now I realize I didn't really know Dick either, though the illusion was always there that I did.

Time passed, and somehow the Marine Corps lost track of Dick's orders, I guess, because the remainder of the four years passed with no more talk of overseas duty. I think I thought now we were safe forever.

I had done what I had to do when I fought for my husband and my baby. Now it is so easy to go back, and wonder—where was Dick, really, in all of this? Did I ever see his needs? Did I

34

ever look close enough? How much do all of us read into each other? Where do the seeds of destruction begin? Of despair begin, of separation?

Dick somehow made it through his four years, was even a captain by the time he left the Marine Corps. Four years of repressing who he really was were over, and yet at night, in the evenings, I believe he was himself then. I believe he could feel joy then, but it's not easy to live a fragmented life.

The strange thing is that I began to want those early years again, and most of all that closeness we had, so much, during the last year before Dick died. Sometimes we would drive fifty miles up the coast to Oceanside, and once there we would go past our little apartment where we had spent Richard's first ten months. I felt almost as if I were trying to catch hold again before it all slipped away.

> Now
> the colors
> of evening
> sift
> through the air.
> Reflections
> from stained glass
> are warm
> as hot tea
> for a moment
> and then
> are gone
> again.

# 2 / Early Days

The Marine Corps faded into our past. Richard grew and thrived. We moved to Livermore, California. We lived there for a year and a half while Dick worked for Lawrence Radiation Lab. It just happened to be the best job he found. A business degree opens doors at large corporations and though that didn't appeal especially to Dick, this job was in Personnel, and he felt that at least in Personnel he would be dealing with people, and Livermore was near San Francisco. We were sure we'd like that.

Life was full, rich, and secure. My home life had always held an element of uncertainty for me, before. During my growing years, my mother's two marriages had never been stable. Now, for the first time, I could depend on "home." Dick liked creating the stability, liked providing for his family. He would tell me this, and he always seemed very proud of us, as if he wanted people to know we were an extension of him.

A year passed. Richard could walk by now. We knew one couple we spent time with on some weekends. I took a watercolor class. Dick didn't say a lot about his job, but life seemed happy and full. Dick's parents came to visit for a while to get acquainted with their first grandchild, and to see us. My mother and stepfather lived in Sacramento, only two hours away. We saw them every month or six weeks.

Then one summer evening, coming home from a walk, Dick and I saw a note tacked on our front door. "Please call this number in Sacramento . . ." It was on police notepaper. I ran in and dialed, then felt blood drain from me as the voice answered, "City Morgue." My mother was there, they said. She had died that morning. An autopsy revealed her death was due to heart failure. It was unbelievable, incredible to me. My mother, fifty-six years old—I'd seen her three weeks before— my mother, whose life was constant unrest, was gone. It was over. The continual anguish she seemed immersed in lately, only sprinkled with bits of joy—the two failed marriages, the frustrations she felt, never able to completely express her music and her life the way she had dreamed—all gone. It always seemed happiness was still waiting for her someplace. Now she was gone. Nothing was ever resolved, I thought. It was just over.

I wished I had been able to say goodbye. I wished I could have hugged her, told her she had been a good mother, that I loved her, but it was too late now.

Earlier that day I had captured a little frog for Richard while he napped. When I went out to show him, the frog was dead. In other losses there have always been other small deaths—and who knows—is the connection only there because we see it?

We drove to Sacramento the next day to take care of funeral plans. My stepfather was shaken. He had just gone to bed before my mother that last night, kissed and left her on the couch watching TV. The next morning he found her, the TV still blaring. I had never been close to my stepfather. There was always so much distress at home, but now I could feel his pain, too. My little grandmother flew out all the way from Oklahoma. At the service she wore a blue dress to match the blue one her daughter would be buried in.

After my mother's death I felt old for a while, felt I was no longer young. I was twenty-eight. I was no one's daughter anymore. I remember that soon after, though, I began to feel a surge of new life. It was a feeling of rebirth. Part of that included the most intense and good time for Dick and for me sexually. Strangely enough I felt very alive. It seems it is easy to let go and take life in when we really face its finiteness.

For Dick and me both, this was our first real experience of being involved with the death of someone close, and it was a very sobering event. Dick was very much with me during that time. Part of my life was gone now. Dick was truly my life. I felt that deeply. He was always very supportive of me. In fact I think he saw his role in just that way, as a sort of protector, but who protected him?

Besides the losses, there were happy times in Livermore—the kites we flew (for Richard, we said, but really for ourselves) in the grassy field near our house—the visits to the wineries and the cheese factories. We loved especially the Wente Winery where at least one Wente brother still lived and worked. Visitors toured the large rooms, saw the immense oak kegs, then sat around a large old table to sample the fine wines and hear the stories of the process—the picking, the crushing. . . .

All during the year, the seasons were reflected in the grapevines growing near the town. When they were dormant, nothing seemed more dead—gnarled, twisted, bent, gray—no sign of life. It was impossible to believe they would ever give forth fruit again, but in a few months, there they would be, lush and green-leaved, heavy bunches of grapes weighing down the new branches and vines.

We often went to San Francisco, and the thrill we felt each time we crossed the bay bridge and saw that magical city before us never diminished. It seemed that city held richness, excitement of thought, humanness, a variety of people and color, old and new, lush green, flowers in unexpected places, the contrast of hills, tight slim houses trying to be as beautiful as possible, and bunched together as if none of them wanted to be left out—and the fog, misting and spreading its way over the city, giving a kind of unity in the diversity. And there were the cherry blossoms in the Japanese garden in Golden Gate Park. We'd have picnics with champagne, and there were the walks through Muir woods, almost a walk in the primitive past, Ghiradelli Square, jazz concerts, trips to Berkeley and to

38

Walnut Creek to see old friends—and I'll never forget the white rabbit that magically appeared in our backyard on Easter.

But our deep wish was to settle back in southern California. Though we had a special love for the physical surroundings in northern California, we felt the southern oceans and beaches draw us, and it was also something more—southern California held a feeling of "home," an unexplainable feeling that San Diego was where we should be.

Dick made inquiries and eventually accepted a job at Teledyne Ryan Aeronautical in San Diego. Richard was two. We moved from our house on Mariposa (butterfly) Street in Livermore, took our dog (Sergeant Pepper) and moved to a rented house in San Diego (on Easy Street). The move went smoothly, and soon we were spending time at the beach, and in general enjoying San Diego.

Dick's job, however, was really no closer to his heart than the Marine Corps. He took it, holding on to the hope that something better would come along. Every morning he would go in to work, kiss me and Richard goodbye and be swallowed by the drab ugly buildings; and many days he would call and ask me if I would bring a picnic lunch and bring Richard down, and we would sit near the water during his lunch break, and just as many times he would ask me to bring meat to barbecue when I picked him up after work, so that we could go to the beach in the evening.

Soon after we settled, we began visiting different churches. Since our marriage we had gone to the Catholic church mostly. It was the church of Dick's boyhood, and we had had Richard baptized in the Old Mission of San Luis Rey in Oceanside. There the rich aura of humanness, of soul and spirit, blended with a mystical feeling which gave a splendor that went beyond the ritual of a church service.

But gradually we found less meaning in the Catholic Church. We decided we would try visiting different ones.

One Sunday morning we happened to go to a Methodist church in San Diego's Mission Valley. After the service we were approached by a thin, bearded man with an English accent, just about our age, late twenties. His name was Mike, he said,

39

and he invited us to come to a young couples' group at the church, called "The Samaritans."

The next Sunday we did just that, and pretty soon we didn't go to the main service anymore; few members of this group did. Our lives were never the same. The meetings marked a turning point in our ways of thinking and relating to people and to ourselves. These people seemed to speak directly to the search in us. It was the beginning of encounter group days. There was participation and sharing. Everyone sat in a circle, and we talked of Maslow, of Carl Rogers, Jung, of ideas and aspirations, intertwined loosely with religion. It was an exciting time, and it was the first time we were ever exposed to the idea of really sharing feelings, not just events. I took to the idea as if I had always been waiting for the opportunity, while Dick was more hesitant, cautious. He was a private person, a person who had never been intentionally revealing of himself.

It wasn't long before fifteen or sixteen of us realized we liked doing art work, and we decided to band together to open a little arts and crafts gallery—more as a place to do our work and to display it than as a place to sell to the public. And yet it became all of that, and more, as our personal lives blended.

Dick was enthusiastic about the project. Just the idea seemed to bring out the creativity in him. He used a lot of this energy in the revamping of the building. We had found a small old wooden frame building in San Diego's Old Town. We knocked down walls, painted the interior and exterior, purchased carpet samples and made a patchwork carpet. We called it "That Gallery." We hung up our work and we opened the doors. People came, bought our work, and we had communication not only among ourselves and our work, but also with others. Nancy's abstract paintings hung on the walls, Dave's metal sculpture added a striking contrast, Josie's delicate baskets sat here and there, holding seashells and her own personal charm, Al's photos captured poetic and stark glimpses of life as he saw it, Betty's woven pillows sat here and there, rustled with beads and shells. All were part of the extended family feeling, and integral with plans for the gallery. Dick did not actively participate by doing work for sale. He later did

40

beautiful stained glass, but I believe those days were a time to perhaps open him to the possibility of his own expression. It was a fairly non-threatening atmosphere to begin to become comfortable with that sort of creativity. That is the way it seemed to me.

Each person, each friend, was reflected in the work of their hands, or in the set-up and atmosphere of the gallery. Most objects were not created specifically "for sale," though they were for sale, but were created out of love and a need for expression. All members had other jobs—several teachers, a minister, a plumber, an architect. This gallery was an avocation to each of us. It held our hearts, and not our business minds.

We took turns keeping the shop open, and we kept a journal which each person wrote in during the time he or she worked in the gallery. It was our continuing letter to ourselves and to each other.

Our gallery meetings were full of plans and promise, of laughter and caring. Sometimes we would meet in small groups, hold encounters, bare our souls, our minds, breaking through our psyches as many people were doing at that time. Dick participated in the groups in the sense that he was present, but not in the sense that he actually shared or opened himself. I remember the way he would sit cross-legged on the floor, and then if someone asked his feelings directly, he would bend his dark hair quickly down and say, "I don't know. You guys are so good at this . . . but I'm just not good at explaining my feelings." The tremor of his voice was somewhat different at those times, as if he genuinely felt slightly threatened.

Recently a friend from those days told me that Dick once, after sitting up half the night talking, confided that he felt afraid of intimacy, that he felt afraid to open himself, to really look within. This was a rare moment of revelation and never happened again. The friend said Dick never again mentioned that night or those feelings. I suppose in some ways we all pay a price for exposing ourselves, but I think the real shame, the real sadness is that that sort of openness is often considered communication, while true communication is so much more. It involves the knowing of the self, and the appropriate,

41

considered sharing of the self with another. It is the I–Thou. Dick didn't need to feel alone in his expression. But he did.

As time went on, most of us drifted from the gallery. Interests changed in the three years we had been involved there, and we began to go our separate ways.

When I look back I realize we were caught up in the new idealism of the late '60s. We were the slightly older flower children, with love and creativity as our gods. It was a close time with our circle of friends. We had never been this close to a group of people before, and never were again, and some of those people are still among the deepest friendships I have. We had interacted in so many ways. Our children played together. We had shared joys and sorrows, and tried to trust one another. Occasionally friends fell in love with friends. We believed everything was basically good, and we tried to see beauty in each other and in life.

As people went their separate ways, several couples divorced. Reality began to set in. Soon only three couples had stayed together. Perhaps this was because we were all looking for something—that we all perhaps were, in a sense, seekers.

Of the three couples who stayed married, one moved back to Texas, another was Catholic, and very family-oriented, and then there were Dick and me—the perfect couple. We had somehow weathered the changes and yet come through together. We didn't OD on love. We had kept our heads and our integrity. The new feelings and awarenesses changed everyone. We had all come together wanting something, and little by little, over the years, we all went our different ways. We learned during that time the joy of creating and expressing ourselves, and of exchanging ideas, feelings, and parts of our lives with a group of people we felt compatible with. Until those days Dick's and my life together was very closed, with only occasional friends. In some ways we hadn't felt a need for others in our life in an intimate way. It was as if we had been living on the outer rim of the egg of the world. Now we had gone down a layer or two into our souls and into more deeply knowing others.

Our family life was still our most prized possession, though, and we both began to feel strongly it was time for another baby. Richard was four. Yet month after month passed, and no pregnancy occurred. We both went to the doctor to see if we had any problems with fertility, but there seemed to be no reason for my inability to conceive.

Finally we went to the adoption agency. Within six months we were called. There was a baby for us—a little girl, six weeks old—tiny, pink, sweet, and soft. We brought her home, named her Marisa. I'll never forget Richard's remark as we drove home that day with Marisa. He hung over the front seat, touching her tiny face and hands, and he said, "Sometimes you wish for something, and it really does come true."

Our friends gave us a shower. Everyone brought gifts for Marisa. Even Dick's parents came from Chicago to see their new grandchild. We both were outwardly happy, but inside I was beginning to be worried. I had just missed my period. The unbelievable had happened. I was pregnant and feared saying anything about it. For weeks I vacillated between depression, "I can't take Marisa back," to anxiety, "I can't have two babies." I was living in torture—could think of nothing else. If I could have accepted two babies—but somehow I couldn't. I just felt overwhelmed. When I told Dick, he became anxious and a little withdrawn, concerned, but not expressive. Not communicative. He seemed always to be working on his turmoil inside, not in an outward way. I never understood the process or knew how to make the contact with his confusion. And so our times of pain were never times of togetherness. We were always separate when we suffered, and more and more I think even joy became separate.

There was often a holding back I sensed in Dick, and I felt it in myself too. I think that when either of us reached out, it was seldom simultaneous, and yet in the good times, it was simultaneous and mutually responsive.

As years go on in a marriage, I wonder, do we become more and more protective of ourselves? As physical intimacy is taken for granted, along with the eggs in the morning, the newspaper at night, dinner, and Johnny Carson, do we all pull into our separate dreams in order not to be lost inside each other's souls? Do we feel we have to hold something back in order not

43

to risk everything? I used to think that sometimes when I had trouble being really close to Dick I probably was afraid to risk it all. I could take other rejection, but not his—and yet, I did lose it all.

The ambivalence about our adopted baby, Marisa, went on. Finally after six weeks I called the agency. They said, "Come in and talk, and remember to bring the baby." We went to her room to dress her, took off her diaper, bathed her in the little yellow tub we had also used for Richard, put a little pink-and-white cotton dress on her and filled the diaper bag with extra diapers. We drove to the agency, and as we came in and sat down to talk to the worker, another woman opened the door. "Let me take the baby for you," she said. "It is easier to talk without her. You can't be objective with her here." I handed Marisa to this woman. "Oh," she said, "Let me take her diaper bag, too, in case we need anything." In a second she was gone. As we talked I told' the caseworker of my confusion and ambivalence, hoping somehow she would say the words to reassure me, or help clear my thoughts. She ended the conversation in a little while by saying they would keep Marisa there at the agency for five days, that this was standard procedure, while they weighed the situation and made a decision. I realized then with horror that it was not to be a mutual decision—that it was to be an "agency decision."

We never saw Marisa again. We were told after those five days that in view of the fact I was expecting a child, and there were many couples waiting for babies, couples who had no children at all and who had no other impediments to adoption, they felt it best to end our adoption proceedings. After all, she said, this was our trial period. I felt then that I knew what it must be like when women have to give up their natural babies soon after birth. We hadn't even had a chance to say goodbye to her, but I know that would have been terribly painful.

It was perhaps best, I thought, but still it was not an easy parting, and was made even more difficult because the decision was not really ours. In my naiveté I had thought we would find counseling there. I felt grief, an aching in my heart. For six weeks she had been our daughter. Now she had no name again. She was back in the pool of anonymity, and would come out again with a new name, a new identity. She would be someone else's daughter. The rational part of me knew she would find another good home, and that we would have our own baby in seven months—and still it hurt. I tried to transfer that energy and turn it into hope and caring for the baby now growing inside me. Dick once again didn't talk much about his own feelings. He said he felt that even if it was hard, it was best. Though he didn't show sadness outwardly I knew he felt it.

The other alternative open to us, besides keeping two babies, would have been abortion, and we were neither of us sure we could handle that. It was just before abortions were legalized, but even so, I would have had my own difficulty with it, I know, though I believe in its being an available choice.

I'll always remember that Marisa had a tiny purple birthmark between the second and third toes on her right foot, and I've always thought that if I ever saw a little girl around her age with that birthmark, I would be able to recognize her.

# 3 / Johanna

The weeks went by, and Dick began searching for another job, something that suited him better than the one at Teledyne Ryan. One day he came home with his news—he'd found a job—one he thought he would really like this time. It, too, was in Personnel. As a matter of fact, now he was categorized as Personnel material, but this job sounded more interesting, challenging, and intriguing, and the surroundings felt right. It was at the University of California. This, he thought, would suit him. He loved the atmosphere of learning and the stimulation of new ideas. He loved also the casualness of the campus. He could just wear wash pants, he would go to noontime concerts, see the art shows, go to the lectures. He could go all over the campus to talk with people—didn't have to stay in the office.

Once in the job he created his own world inside the office. He set out photos of me and Richard, hung up several of my watercolors and a large drawing by Richard. Anytime a friend gave him a little picture, or something to set around, that, too, went into the office; and plants—he had seven or eight, different varieties which he carefully tended—all to the tune of

46

his FM radio, which his boss one day caught him dancing to.

Things began to seem right and good. At home we waited for the birth of our second child, and were very involved with our friends, the gallery, and each other. Richard missed Marisa. He had been so happy when she came home with us. We said to Richard, "We'll have our own baby soon—just wait." And we did wait. We busied ourselves with plans now for our new baby, for Richard's brother or sister. I redid the bassinet with new white eyelet. We painted the nursery orchid and light green. Everything seemed right: work, family life, friendships.

I felt totally full of life and love—made Christmas presents for everyone we cared about, watercolors and paintings that suited each special friend.

And in December, three days before Christmas, 1970, Johanna Leigh Kenyon was born.

In the delivery room the doctor congratulated me—a nine-pound baby girl, and she has all her fingers and toes, he said. I was thrilled, could hardly believe it. Too good to be true, I felt. I cast a fleeting glance at my baby as they whisked her from the room to an isolette. A breathing problem, they said.

In a little while the pediatrician came into the recovery room. She asked my age and if I'd had any problems with the pregnancy. I was thirty-one, and it had been an easy, carefree pregnancy with no problems, I told her.

These questions seemed a little strange, but otherwise she said nothing out of the ordinary. I tried to put the glimmer of worry from my mind. After all, what could be wrong?

As time went on, though, I perceived a discernible difference as I contrasted the attitude of these nurses and hospital people with their attitude after Richard was born. There were no congratulations with Johanna—no smiling strangers standing at my door saying, "I heard you had a beautiful baby," or "I just saw your little one . . ."

I recall one nurse came in, and as she straightened things up, she said, "Do you have any other children? . . . Is he healthy?"

Distance and separation hung in the air.

When you have a healthy child, you are praised. Everyone smiles. If your baby is not perfect, you can sense it. Joy is missing. Contact with others is missing. I felt isolated. No one knew what to say. By the next day I was frightened. When my doctor came in to check me, I asked, "Is something wrong with my baby?"

"Let's not jump to conclusions," he said. "We try to be very careful. We're just checking to be certain she is really OK." Then he added, "I'm almost sure she is."

After he left I walked down to look at Johanna. She looked fine. She was kicking her legs and moving her arms. Her eyes were open and she was looking around. Her hair was dark like Dick's. I imagined her as a little girl, a pretty little girl with long black hair, Johanna Leigh, Richard's little sister. She's got to be OK, I thought.

I tried to still the anxiety inside. Back in my room, though, it wouldn't be quieted. I called Dick. "Will you come?" I said. "I'm afraid something might be wrong with our baby. Something doesn't feel right." I started to cry. He said he'd come. I tried to keep working on the Christmas card announcements I had made to send friends and relatives—a series of cutout stars, connected by string. On the stars I wrote a couple of lines from e. e. cummings: "love is the every only god/who spoke this earth so glad and big." On the last star I wrote: Johanna Leigh Kenyon, 9 lbs., 5 oz., December 22, 1970.

In a little while Dick came into the room and tried to reassure me. "Karen, you always worry about everything. I'm sure she is fine," he said.

Only minutes later the pediatrician walked in briskly. "Your baby is out of the isolette," she said. "She doesn't have a breathing problem anymore, but we are fairly sure she is— mongoloid."

The word cut like a knife. I covered my face in unacceptance. It seemed unbelievable. Dick just dropped his head in his lap and began to cry. He seemed totally shaken. The only times I recall seeing Dick weep were in relation to Johanna.

I discovered two weeks later, through blood tests, that I had always carried within me the possibility of giving birth to a Down's syndrome baby.* It was hard to realize and accept this, but it is a reality. Perhaps the first baby I miscarried was also a Down's. I'll never know, and it doesn't really matter.

*Down's syndrome children have 47 chromosomes, rather than the normal 46. In a case of translocation, which was the reason for Johanna's mongolism, either mother or father carries a double chromosome—two chromosomes

48

Now, years later, I wonder why we always have to see such children as tragedies. And yet, it hurts so much to know a child is not healthy, and that we will likely lose it one day. Dick and I both felt grief for the loss of the child we expected, and we both learned to love the child we had been given, and yet it wasn't easy.

The nurse finally brought Johanna to me, soon after the doctor left. It was the first time I held her. I was still shocked. Who was she? I thought. I felt I didn't know her. Though she did not look unusual to me in any way, the label she now wore was stronger than anything my senses could perceive. This was not the baby I expected, I told myself, not the baby we had painted the nursery and decorated the bassinet for. I felt strange and unreal. Hurt covered my heart, so that I could not feel, could not give love to my baby who needed love. I think now that perhaps if she had been bonded to me, that is, if I had been allowed to hold her immediately after delivery, she would have been first of all my baby, my child, and secondly, a Down's syndrome baby. I rang for the nurse to take her back, and all I could think was that I wanted to go home.

The world had been turned upside down. The promises didn't come true, and no one had warned me.

We had to remake the phone calls to our families, telling them we didn't have a healthy baby after all. And then I called friends, almost as if I thought someone along the line would say, No, that isn't true.

I was released from the hospital before Johanna. She had to stay for further tests. Dick picked me up and we came home to the Christmas tree, and to Richard, wanting to know where his baby sister was.

The day after Christmas we returned to the hospital to pick up Johanna and to bring her home. The nurse just handed her to me, and said, "Here she is. She drinks and wets and everything." That was all. Suddenly we were handed a bundle

"stuck together," appearing as one. If this chromosome is given to the fetus, the baby will have an extra chromosome and be born mongoloid. This means the child will have a lower than average intelligence and any number of physical problems, including poor muscle tone and heart problems. The life span is shorter than the average person's.

49

of life we knew had special needs, but which we didn't really understand. We were in no way prepared psychologically for a handicapped child. We later called a psychologist friend, who made calls and eventually got us in touch with Regional Center for the Developmentally Disabled. There we found help and information. We learned she had no special needs now, other than what any baby needs—love, food and care. We also learned, though, that Down's babies do not often cry and so you need to anticipate their hunger and feed them on schedule. They don't ask for much. We learned some of what we might expect in the future, and we learned more about the biological reasons for the syndrome. On a personal level, the Regional Center felt like home, for people there understood our dilemma. They gave us understanding and resources for help, and they called Johanna by her name. The doctors there didn't refer to her as "the baby" as all the other doctors had.

Richard was thrilled when we brought Johanna home. His vision was' unclouded by labels or names. She was his baby sister, and he loved her. He put toys in her bassinet when we first brought her into the house. She made him happy from the start. Johanna always smiled when Richard came near.

And our close friends helped. They held her, gave her presents and love. They accepted her. In general, though, there is in the world much unacceptance, and I often felt a need for explanation, and I felt shame and guilt. I soon realized, however, I didn't need to tell people about her. If someone saw us in a store and said, "What a cute baby," instead of my guilt saying, "Thank you, but she is Down's syndrome," I would just say "Thank you." That seemed complete. She was cute, and someone appreciated her. That was all that mattered. Though I may have been wrong I didn't tell babysitters anything was wrong with Johanna. They thought she was precious and sweet and they loved her, so I didn't want them to feel saddened, and I didn't want to possibly deny her their love. It didn't seem necessary to cast a different light on her.

There was beauty in Johanna, but because of my hurt I came to my love for her slowly. I recall, though, just a few days after we brought her home how touched I felt by her. I put her across my shoulder to burp her after a feeding, and she was

50

trying with all her might to hold her head up. The drive for life and growth was there. It amazed me, and seemed even more beautiful than it would have seemed in a normal child.

It was several weeks before I could really know deeply that I loved her. I like to sketch, and one day I drew her. As I looked closely and carefully I began to truly drink Johanna in. I couldn't hold the love back then. Sometimes I wonder why it took so long, and yet I'm glad it did finally become clear.

Johanna's smiles were precious and beautiful. She smiled within a few weeks. She even learned to turn from her stomach to her back, and once actually rolled from her back to her stomach.

Dick seemed very involved with Johanna. He accepted her totally right away. He filled in the gap I had felt for her initially. He loved her from the start. He was hurt, too, but, "She is our little baby," he said. "It shouldn't have happened to us, but it shouldn't have happened to her either." Soon, though, we both just felt—why shouldn't it have happened to us? Or rather, it couldn't have happened any other way.

We began to love her for what she was, rather than for what she wasn't, and as I began to truly feel this, I wrote this poem for her.

### For Johanna

Will you see the butterfly
better because you won't
wonder where he came from?

Will the flowers be brighter
because you won't have to
know their names?

Will you be able to trust
completely in today because
you will have no worries about tomorrow?

And will the world be a better place
because of you?

51

Becase you will not learn to hate,
and you will not make war,
and you will not hold life to its promises,
because it didn't give you any.

And you will be a part of everything,
You will be the butterfly,
You will be the flower,
And I will let you be all of this in me.

(originally printed in
*Ladies' Home Journal,* November, 1974)

But our days with Johanna were short. She left as unexpectedly as she had come. One night when Johanna was six months old, as I started to fall asleep next to Dick and was in that state between sleep and wakefulness when the subconscious mind often surfaces, I began to have the feelings I thought I would experience if she were to die. I knew someday she would, for I had been told in all probability she would not grow up. I always pictured this happening at around age five. But that night the feelings came, and all I could think was— Oh, I can't bear it—how will I bear it?

The next night we were at our friends Christy and Larry's house for coffee after a basketball game. Richard was asleep on the couch. Johanna was in her carbed on our friends' bed. I went in to get her, but she was already gone. Dick gave her mouth-to-mouth resuscitation. He always seemed to know exactly what to do to help, and to give this help calmly and skillfully. A police car drove us to the hospital. I heard the policeman say on his car radio, "A baby is not breathing," and I thought, "a baby," not "a baby who is not normal." Just "a baby." She was equal then.

At the hospital they worked on her for over an hour, but it was too late.

The doctor came out to tell us and to ask if we wanted to see her. We walked in and saw her lying on the cold steel table. She looked like a little doll. I pushed a lock of hair off her forehead for the last time, and Dick bent down and kissed her.

I remember the young doctor had tears in his eyes. I looked

at him and said, "We didn't even have her baptized." He said simply, "I baptized her."

An autopsy was later performed. No cause of death was found, and so she was termed a victim of Sudden Infant Death syndrome. Later her heart specialist told us that in cases of Down's syndrome the conductive system between the brain and the heart is weak, and that in all probability her brain didn't give her heart the message to beat.

The day she was buried our friends came to the little graveside ceremony. Someone read my poem for her. Another friend played a Spanish lullaby on his guitar. Flowers from people's yards were placed near the little white box—daisies and roses with ribbons.

We didn't let Richard come to the service. We thought he was too young, and that it wouldn't be good for him. I believe now we should have. He has told me several times through the years he wished he had been able to go. I guess it would have made the parting more real to him. Even children have the right and need to be able to say goodbye. Later I learned that Richard and his friends found a small doll they thought looked like Johanna. They buried the doll in the friend's yard. I guess it is still there.

When we came home, we closed the door to her room. It was too hard to go in. The smell of baby powder filled the air.

A beautiful golden hibiscus bush that flourished outside her nursery window died, soon after Johanna left.

I began to take Richard to the park a lot. Being outside seemed to help. Dick went back to his job, and life just went on.

The world's attitude toward the death of someone judged imperfect is that "It was all for the best." The hurt is there, and the loss, but in some ways this attitude makes it harder to work through the grief.

When I called to tell my brother Johanna had died, I said, sobbing, "Bud, my baby died." He said, "Well, Karen, how do you feel about that?" And all I could say was, "I loved her." And then he said, "I'm sorry, Karen."

Dick and I did not cling to one another in this grief. Maybe it was just too much, too close. Instead we both sought our own way to deal with what had happened.

Maybe I could express my grief easier than Dick could. I cried a lot. I put pictures of her away for a while, and it was hard for me to be around anyone with a baby, but after a while I wrote about Johanna. The story, her story, was published in *Redbook* (March, 1972). By doing this I not only had a catharsis, but I had transformed the event by showing the order and beauty and sense.

After that I returned to college to study writing. A new path had opened for me, but Dick's day-to-day life was much the same. I had more of an outlet for my grief, and I guess he really didn't. I wonder now how it truly affected him. I know there was little acknowledgement of the blot on his life, the loss he had suffered. When a child dies, I think too often it is the mother who is comforted, and the father's job is seen as that of comforting the mother.

Things began to change subtly between us. There had been closeness in the joy of Richard. There seemed to be separation in the sadness of Johanna. We both bore our pain inside and sought separate outlets. For me the feeling of family unity was less, but the feeling of openness to the world was more.

I think, in all honesty, there is, along with the sadness of the unwellness of a child, a blow to the ego. The truth is that so much is available to learn from such a child, about love, about ourselves—but we are taught that only our beautiful children reflect our goodness. When our children are less than what is judged perfect we then see our own feeling of imperfection reflected, as if that part is there for all the world to see, and we are exposed. I, who perhaps could not be so honest with my sense of unwholeness, which I think all of us have, had to see her as whole, complete within herself, and then I could identify with her. So I gradually drew strength from Johanna. I began to feel we are all handicapped, and whole too, in some ways—only it just shows more on some. I felt a oneness with all people and with all afflictions, at least for a time. In some ways I think Dick related to Johanna through her unwholeness, seeing the unexpressed, unknown parts of himself in her.

Johanna was a baby who taught us love. Instead of praying for perfect children, perhaps we should pray for a child who can teach us love. She was a wonderful gift, marked at first by

54

our conception of beauty and normalcy, while true beauty lay beneath.

That was eight years ago. After Dick died I talked one day to a secretary on the campus where he had worked. I had heard Dick did speak to her often, especially in his last weeks.

The woman told me she had lost her daughter in a car wreck a few years ago, and then she had wanted to commit suicide to "join her"—said she had driven her car over a cliff at one point, but the car caught on a tree stump. Realizing then this was wrong, she said she began to feel she was supposed to live, so she never tried it again. She had told Dick all about this.

She relayed to me that Dick had told her he was beginning to have thoughts again about Johanna, waves of grief, and he said that this, coupled with stresses on his job, was almost too much. He told her he didn't want to bring all this unhappiness, especially the work problems, home to Richard and to me.

He asked her, she said, "Do you think this is false pride?"

So, it was clear, he had tried to keep the feelings inside, and yet where else should they have lived, if not at home? Dick had wanted to protect too much. He knew we loved him, but maybe that love meant too much responsibility. And I suppose he had no confidence he could really lean on me, or anyone, that there was "home" in that sense. Perhaps he carried too much love and protection for us, too much pride, and not enough love for himself. How will I ever know if I would have failed him or helped him?

I wish that, of all the people Dick could have talked to, he had chosen someone who could have pushed him toward life. I know he must have identified with this woman. Though she gave up on thoughts of ending her life, she did understand those feelings. Even though he did not tell her specifically about his thoughts of suicide, he must have felt a strange comfort in the sharing with her.

Two things I learned from her. Dick hadn't finished with his feelings about Johanna, and there was a part of him that never really came home to me. Maybe no two people really know one another, can really rest their souls in each other totally.

55

# 4 / Hotel California

Welcome to the Hotel California
Such a lovely place (such a lovely face)
They livin' it up at the Hotel California
What a nice surprise, bring your alibi. . . .

And she said, "We are all just prisoners here,
of our own device. . . ."

The years after Johanna's death were full of the California
good life. We lived a life full of friends, of the new psychol-
ogies. We went to extension courses, a few encounter groups,
we sat in Jacuzzis. We went to art shows, to Shakespeare in the
park, to concerts. It seemed we had the best of everything, but
now I think something was missing—the birth and loss of
Johanna seemed to create a space between us. In this space
grew a search for more separate identity.

During this time Dick continued work at UCSD and I
finished going back to college, wrote articles. We went to
parties and gatherings. Outwardly we seemed to have a perfect

life. Dick was intelligent, with a sense of humor, and was well-liked. I wrote and did some art work, some batik. Dick always seemed proud of me, and encouraged me. We had a beautiful young boy, Richard, and we had weathered and triumphed over the pain of Johanna. While our friends' marriages all broke up, ours endured. Everyone seemed a little in awe of us. We didn't seem to need anything. Apparently we were handling everything.

But the fairy tale was slipping.

After Johanna's death, there were feelings of failure and of loss. I craved to fill the gap left, and as I filled it with school, writing, and new friends, I became more independent. As I wrote more stories and experienced the world more, a feeling for life was beginning for me which I could never truly communicate to Dick, though I tried. My newfound knowledge didn't come from Dick, though certainly it was born of the relationship we shared, but we had both learned and grown now in our own different ways. I was on a voyage of self-discovery, beginning to have my own dream. For the first time in my life, I felt some ambition, not in the sense of being a "success" but in the sense of doing work I could feel involved in and care about. Now the world had once again shifted.

Dick began to find his own new interests. He began to go scuba diving. He loved to plunge deep into the sea. He loved the beauty—the gently swaying kelp and the graceful movement of the fish. Richard drew a picture, which Dick promptly hung in his office. It was "My Daddy—Diving."

After awhile Dick began to do stained glass work. He seemed to find a lot of joy in this, and the pieces he did were exquisite. During this time he also began to grow a beard and mustache and from then on he always had at least a mustache.

An ability and interest in decorating the house grew and bloomed within Dick during these days. He would often work late into the night, sometimes until three or four in the morning, putting up wall coverings, tiling the entryway. His craftsmanship was impeccable, and he worked unceasingly. He seemed to lose awareness of time when he was deeply involved. I remember that when he tiled the front bathroom he worked on it regularly and late into the nights for one year. It was as perfect as humanly possible.

As a contrast, at the university, time was important. At work so many things had to be completed, one upon another, by a certain date, and his decisions had to please those who held rank above him in the university system. When he used his creativity at home, though, the decisions were his alone. He had a very justifiable pride in what he did, and he seemed to gain pleasure from his accomplishments. More and more our house became a personal statement of Dick, and in a lesser way, of me, too.

We began to have parties. People seemed to love to come to our house. Happy memories began to fill in the little space where the lost flower had fallen through.

And yet we were beginning to split apart gradually the way a fertilized egg begins to divide. Though still a part of one another, we were not completely separate and discrete. We still slept together, near one another, but often with our backs toward each other. It was as if in some way we were missing the creative heart of our life together. We were lacking a common purpose, perhaps. We were not both sharing in something we cared about. I don't know. I think there is some truth here, and yet—I grasp now for straws. I know I took a lot for granted when it came to Dick—did not have a newborn appreciation each day, not the mixture of fear, joy, and courage that comes from the risk of dropping truly into new love, and knowing we have given up parts of ourselves to one another. I feel we had slowly been taking back parts of ourselves. I know I had. And yet it always seemed to me we were basically close. I always felt we were bound up with one another, meant to be together. Any growth or changes I experienced were always based in Dick. I assumed he felt the same way.

Dick's job at UCSD continued. It involved mediating disputes about salary increases. From what I now know people always wanted more than he was able to give them. He was often caught in the middle of conflict, and his own human

58

values often conflicted with university policy. He spoke little of the frustration, but I knew something of the way so many of his decisions were thwarted. Not much room for his creativity and compassion existed, and as he was forced to handle an increasingly larger group of employees, less and less time could be spent doing a careful job, and this was essential to him.

He sought release more and more in scuba diving. When he dove he felt at peace, and by doing stained glass he could use his expression, his choice, and his care.

More and more he would say, "God, I can't stand that job. I wish some days I worked for McDonald's!" And then he would apply for something a little different from his job in Personnel. He wanted out of the conflict, but the answers to his applications were always, "But you are qualified for Personnel—we can't risk hiring someone who doesn't have specific experience in our vacant position." He was beginning to feel trapped.

And I seemed to need him less and less in the old ways, as protector, and yet needed him in new ways, as an equal. We were in a time of transition, of change.

Yet outwardly we did not make changes in our life. We talked of trips we would take, but we never went farther than San Francisco, Los Angeles, or Tijuana for a day or two— never Cabo San Lucas, where Dick wanted to go diving, never made real plans to go to Greece, where we both wanted to travel someday. Our life continued in the same house, with Dick in the same job and Richard at the same school. We were stable. We were stuck.

We did not seek material goods and status and yet we wanted to enjoy our life, and we liked our home to reflect us. We liked to think we stood outside of surface goals—we were looking for something more. We sought quality of friendships, of artistry and learning. I always thought of our way as finely chosen.

During this time, however, it began to feel to me that a space was growing in our hearts. I sensed this. I began to feel a desire to draw back—to each other—to "home."

I'd gone back to college, had a small career. Now I could feel our house starting to shatter a bit, and I wanted to bind it up, to feel intimacy, to use the power I felt I still had, to have a child, as if that was the answer. Had I forgotten I still had the power to love?

The life of ever-available instant enlightenment, of hot tubs, lectures, and friends, began to grow stale, and in time we drew away from most friends. I think in some ways there was a feeling of disillusion. When Dick died I realized all the outside "answers" hadn't been an answer to his life—all the available therapy, the friends, all the California solutions. All the Jacuzzis, all the "evolved" people, and circumstances in the world hadn't saved him, or maybe any one could have, if it had been taken deep enough.

Dick didn't die because he didn't know all the help available, all the alternatives available. We lived in the middle of all possibilities. He worked in the middle of all possibilities. But his questions and his answer came from within.

Just three months before his death he needed to go to the University of California at Irvine for two days for his job. Dick realized that Laguna Beach was not far from Irvine, and that in Laguna Beach a small hotel actually existed called Hotel California. He had liked the song by the Eagles for months, often playing it with the earphones on, excluding the world. He said he wanted to stay there in the hotel. When I said I could come, too, he said, "Why don't you and Richard just ride the train up—the second day—and we'll have dinner—and all drive home together?" This idea wasn't like Dick. Ordinarily he would have wanted me to go with him. I felt he must need that privacy, that aloneness.

He did stay in the Hotel California. I don't know how he spent his free time. Was he happy or sad there? What did he contemplate in his time alone?

As the train pulled up for a stop in the little beach town with Richard and me, there was Dick, as planned, waiting for us near the pier.

> Last thing I remember, I was
> Running for the door
> I had to find the passage back

To the place I was before
"Relax," said the night man,
"We are programmed to receive,
You can check out anytime you like,
but you can never leave."

# 5 / Birth and Death

Birth and death. Beginnings and endings. Endings and beginnings.

It is so ironic when I think that eight years after Johanna I was struggling for a new beginning just as another ending was waiting.

When Johanna died I didn't have the courage or desire to take the risk and try for another baby. Dick agreed it was hazardous, but now I felt willing to take the dare.

I don't think I ever, inside, let go of the fantasy of having another baby. It was just something I put away consciously. I think, too, that when a baby dies, your arms never forget the way that baby felt, and physically you yearn for your arms to be full again. They are so suddenly emptied. You can keep the baby in your heart and in your mind, but you miss the feeling of tiny soft life against your skin. So, I believe my grief wasn't completely resolved, and that Dick's wasn't either.

My brother (who also carries the translocated chromosome) married. He and his wife, Marcia, within a couple of years, had two beautiful baby girls—perfect physically and mentally. My heart began to yearn again for the baby I had lost, and

I thought this would give us new life—something joyful. I had begun to notice Dick and Richard, anytime they were around children or babies. They both shared the wonderful ability to genuinely love little children and to abandon themselves to play. Dick could out-play any child—he was wonderful to watch with children. He intimately involved himself with them.

I watched Dick and Richard on the beach one day, playing with Cara, my friend Christy's two-year-old child. I saw Dick playfully chase her, and I saw Richard pick her up and hug her, and I could see then how much they were both missing, and how much they could give. And I wanted to give this experience to them, for their own. I felt guilty, in fact, that I had held back for so long.

I was thirty-nine. I knew my days were numbered, as far as bearing children—that it was now or never. I knew it wasn't the best time as far as my age went, but I knew some time remained. It wasn't too late. It's strange because I believe now it was the sense of something about to be lost—the pulling away I sensed in Dick. My attempt to give birth was in part my attempt to hold onto life—our life.

I asked Dick what he thought about a child. He had always loved babies and children. I always thought he was disappointed we didn't have more. He replied, rather flatly, "I think it would be a good idea." I asked him over and over. I wanted to be sure. I felt this should be what we both wanted, and I felt I needed his support very much. It was risky. I didn't want to feel alone. But I felt hopeful. Until then I had accepted the fact we would have no more children. Now I felt that could be changed.

Within a few months I did become pregnant. In fact I think I could tell the very day. I felt so sensitive to my body. That slightly different physical sensation was something I was aware of almost immediately. It gave me a wonderful thrilled feeling. I loved the little speck of life in me, and I felt totally complete, happy and joyful. I told Dick I was fairly sure I was pregnant. He wasn't sure I really knew—said I should wait for the test. In a few weeks the test confirmed what by then I knew.

But Dick didn't act thrilled as I thought he would. I thought he would be happy. I thought he would become stronger and more protective, the way he had before in other pregnancies. I wanted him to be pleased, to be proud of himself, and to be strong enough to carry both of us through. I know that was asking a lot. I guess even more I thought this baby would bring us closer together—bind us and Richard too—and in many ways give new life to our family. I had wanted something wonderful to happen. This was perhaps not the best reason to conceive a child, for this baby was conceived out of hope, and not just out of love. I was reaching for a miracle.

Dick began to change even more—almost imperceptibly at first, but it grew more and more evident—not the happy change I had expected, but a withdrawal, a disappearance of the self.

So I was living in my world of hope and thoughts of new life, fearing the four-and-a-half-month midpoint when I could have an amniocentesis (testing of the amniotic fluid to determine if the baby was normal genetically), but experiencing the life in me at the time, while Dick seemed to fade away. We began to grow separate at the time I had thought we would grow closer together.

Richard, on the other hand, was very happy. He reacted the way I thought Dick would. He whispered to me—could he tell his friends? I said, "Richard, we don't know yet if the baby will be all right." I had explained to him about the amniocentesis, even told him about my misgivings, but said we would just wish for the best. I told him, too, that I almost didn't tell him the news at all because if it didn't work out, I didn't want him to be disappointed. He said, "Mom, even if we don't actually have the baby, I at least want to be happy about it now."

So, Richard, a child, and I, slightly full of child, dreamed of new life, and Dick, I know now, began to dream of death.

The days went by, and I began to feel more ill than I had with other pregnancies. I had just started a half-day job at the university, and had just begun teaching a night class in writing in my home. I couldn't let any of these people know yet, and I had to act as if I felt fine. I guess I didn't spend a lot of time thinking about how Dick was. I was, I suppose, becoming self-contained, and somewhat unattainable to him, just at a time

64

when he truly needed me. We were both becoming locked into our own worlds—unable to reach across.

The stage was being set.

I know now he was disappearing slowly. He was socially dying, and I wasn't realizing, wasn't seeing, what was happening. I knew he was unresponsive and withdrawn. I was hurt that he didn't seem to care about the baby. I felt angry that he was so distant from me. I asked him if it was the baby, and I also asked him if it was me. He said, "No, Karen, I'm just a little inward," or once he said, "No, it's my job, OK?"

He only spoke in sentences, not in paragraphs.

Perhaps if I hadn't been so concerned with myself I could have seen more clearly. I knew something was wrong, but I didn't know what, and he said very little to me.

Dick had always seemed so stable, it was impossible to even imagine the thoughts he must have had. He was the last person on earth I could ever have dreamed would take his life. Everything he did was pro-life. He gave blood at the blood bank. He wanted his organs donated when he died. He took a CPR course. He believed in life, and he believed in sharing and not wasting ourselves.

But I know now, as he said in his last letter, "something snapped," inside his mind. Something in him changed. I believe now someone in a suicidal state is on a completely different level of consciousness, and it is pointless and even dangerous for us to try to grasp and understand that later. Yet, now I feel if Dick had a fatal flaw, I believe it was his need to protect, to be "perfect," and to endure. At this time in his life elements were present which taken to the extreme would soon lead to his destruction.

In early October I began to have some bleeding. The doctor told me to keep off my feet, stay in bed until it stopped. Then if it stopped I could get up. It was difficult—the October heat was sweltering. I stayed on the couch in the living room with the fan on me for days. The bleeding stopped intermittently. When it did we would go for a ride in the car, or a little walk in the park, and then it would start again. I became depressed. I recall saying if I had to live this way, I wouldn't want to live at all—that it would be better to have one wonderful day, doing

65

whatever I wished, than to live like this. Now I wonder why, why I said it. It was just dialogue to me. But Dick must have been slowly building a case for his death, and so what I said probably fit right in.

In general, Dick seemed more present and supportive during those two weeks when I threatened miscarriage than he had before. He seemed to rally somewhat. I guess because he felt he was needed. But I also recall Mike, Richard's friend, coming in one evening and saying, "What's the matter with Mr. Kenyon? He doesn't come out in the street to play ball with us anymore?"

On the evening of October 13, cramping started. Not bad, but it worried me. I later went to sleep. The relaxation of my body probably relieved the pain, but I awakened fitfully around 4:00 A.M. and it was stronger. I lay quietly, but the cramps only increased in intensity, so that by 7:00 A.M. or so, I knew I had to call the doctor. She said to come to the emergency room at the hospital in an hour, that she would be in a meeting, but could be called out.

When I lay back on the bed my water broke, and I knew we should leave. Dick was kind and helpful. He took care of me, the way he always had when I needed help. Richard went to a friend's house for the day.

Soon after we arrived I was put in an examining room to wait. Lying on the cold table with only a sheet, I trembled, had pains, and bled so much I began to fear I would pass out. I watched the door, and when a nurse walked past it, I called to her, "Could you send for a doctor?" Soon a doctor came, assisted me, pressing on my uterus. Out came all that was left of my pregnancy. It must have died a few weeks ago, she said.

I didn't want to cry. I tried biting it back. I asked for Dick. He came in and sat down. His eyes were soft and sad.

"Do you know?" I said.

He nodded.

It felt as if a silent stone fell between us.

The doctor said I needed a D and C—to be sure the placenta was out too. She sent me, and Dick with me, to another floor. For a few minutes my gurney was placed in a small, cold, dark room. Dick was still standing near. I recall I became afraid of death then. I almost said it felt like a morgue in there—but I didn't, afraid to throw on so ominous a light.

When they pushed me down the hall, I remember saying to Dick as we parted, "I love you," and I remember feeling that if I didn't say it, it wouldn't be said, and I wanted to be sure to have spoken those words in case I never saw him again. But I had no logical reason to feel that way.

I came home later that day. Dick took care of me as I rested, but he didn't spend time with me. He brought me a glass of juice—then a cup of tea—and then left the room.

Richard was sorry about the baby.

"Richard," I said, "maybe Dad and I will try again. We know now we can do it."

But he only shook his head. "No, Mom. I don't think you should. It'll get to be just like the hamsters." We had had three different hamsters, and each one died. Finally Richard didn't want any more hamsters.

"Pretty soon," he said, "we won't care anymore." He was twelve years old, but he already knew about loss and disappointment. He wanted a baby brother or sister, but he knew it was almost too much to ask.

Later, Bonnie, Mike's mother, took Richard to the shopping center. Soon he walked in my room grinning and holding a vase with three carnations. This touched me. The card said, "Get well soon—Love, Richard, and Mike, and Mike's Mom." But Dick didn't bring me a flower. That is the one thing that sticks in my mind so much now. He had always brought me flowers before. But not this time—not one flower. This was not like him. He always did that kind of tender, loving thing. After all, a flower is a sign of life.

The next day I was up, and wanting to be hopeful, probably trying to not feel my grief, I said to Dick, "What do you think about trying again in a few months?"

He said simply and without emotion, "It'll all work out." He was in bed at the time, and he stayed there all day and half of the next day.

This was strange, and I felt concerned. I said to him, "Maybe you are physically sick. Why don't you see Dr. Bailey?"

"Oh, I'm OK."

But I knew he wasn't. "Well. I'll call and make an appointment for a check-up for you."

He turned over in bed and closed his eyes. "No, I'll do it later on."

I regret that sometime during that day, when I came into the room and he put up his arms for me to kiss him and hold him, I only briefly hugged him. I didn't know what kind of sickness he had, and I thought it was probably the flu. I was tired of not feeling good. I didn't want to be sick with flu on top of everything else. And yet he needed love. That was more important. But I didn't give it to him that day. Maybe he wanted to hold on to life. But I didn't know.

There are so many times we hold back love as if we have forever. I could have given love then, but I didn't.

Toward the end of that day I went out to the grocery store. When I returned, he said, "My mother called."

"Oh," I said, "what did she say?"

"Just that Kathy (Dick's sister) had a baby girl a few days ago, and when I told her we had lost ours, she said she was sorry."

"Oh." I didn't know what to say—and then I noticed his downcast look. "How did it make you feel?"

"Like some people can do it, and some can't."

I didn't want him to say that—didn't want to feel defeated myself.

"Why should you feel bad?" I said. "If anyone should feel bad, it should be me. It wasn't your fault."

The sands were quickly dropping in the hourglass that was our life. There wasn't going to be much more time—about two weeks. That's all. A crazy runaway train was heading toward our lives—only I couldn't see it, couldn't hear it. When I lost that baby, perhaps the clusters of circumstances now living in Dick like nested psychic icons, making him exceedingly vulnerable, opened one into the other, and everything pointed to conclusion—no hope, no room for him. I was grasping frantically for life, and he was reaching for death—and we were blind to one another.

The day passed. He didn't call the doctor. The next afternoon he got out of bed, and he went to work.

# RAIN

Hope
is not so much
seeking the rainbow,

as it is
not being afraid
to look at the rain.

(1971)

69

# 6 / The Ending

On Saturday, October 28, we went to a Halloween party given by a newspaper in town for which I had written. Dick didn't seem to care about going. He seemed increasingly distracted. He said he didn't know what to wear. At one point he said, "Maybe I'll wear the holster and gun I used to have in college."

I thought this was strange. He hadn't mentioned that gun in years and years.

"We don't even know where it is, do we?" I said.

He didn't pursue the idea. Finally we left for the party, in just a hodgepodge of old clothes we'd found around the house. As we drove, he looked at me and said, "You look so pretty." I didn't know why he said it. I just had on funny Halloween clothes. Now I know he was seeing life with the new eyes people develop before they die. Everything is seen in its true beauty, clarity, and richness.

On Sunday, the twenty-ninth, I gave a Halloween party for Richard. Dick just kind of went along with me in the planning. At one point he stood up on a canvas chair to hang up streamers. When the chair split from his weight, he said, "Why did I do that? It was so stupid."

I said, "Well, those things happen."

And he said, "But it was so stupid."

I felt an odd uneasiness inside. It was very unlike Dick to do anything that was in any way careless, though it was like him to be hard on himself if he felt he somehow didn't come up to his own expectations. I could see he was almost frightened by this slight misjudgment. But we set up the party, and it felt good to have this task to accomplish. I thought—Later Dick and I will have a party. We needed to see friends. We had not been as involved with friends the last months or year.

Richard's party was wild and fun. I hired a magician who did wonderful tricks of illusion with scarves and fire, accompanied by taped exotic music. The kids played all their favorite music, ate hot dogs, drank Cokes, bobbed for apples, voted on the best costume. It was a great success.

Dick was around, and he helped during the party, but it was beginning to feel like I was living with a whisper for a person.

That was Sunday.

Monday night I went to a movie with a friend from work, Catherine. I didn't usually go out with friends without Dick, but I wanted to see the movie *Stevie*, the story of the poet, Stevie Smith, and so did Catherine. Dick didn't seem interested.

It was excellent, I thought, well done, starring Glenda Jackson. Stevie Smith did commit suicide, and though this was not shown in the movie, her thoughts were, "If all else fails you in life, you always can count on your old friend, death."

The thought was interesting to me on an intellectual level. Suffering doesn't have to go on forever. It was an abstract thought I toyed with in my mind, after the movie—an expression to be discussed. I told Dick about the movie, and about her philosophy. I was used to telling him all my thoughts. Now I know we don't always realize the messages we may be conveying. I am much more careful these days of words and thoughts. I wonder too about the synchronicity of it all. Why, of all movies? Why, of all thoughts? It's as if it was in the air.

72

I suppose to Dick it just fit in, and maybe he even thought it would help me understand. In his note he said he had thought of suicide for months.

The next night was Halloween—Tuesday. I stayed home, built a fire in the fireplace, and handed out the treats while Dick went around with Richard for "trick or treat." So we weren't together and didn't talk much that night.

Wednesday night, November 1, All Saints' Day. That night I had a writing class which I taught in our house. That meant the living room was taken over by students, and that once again we had little time to be together.

Thursday, November 2, All Souls' Day. I went to work and it was planned I would come to Dick's office when I was through for the day, after 1:00 P.M. I was going first to talk with Dodie, an employment interviewer in Dick's office. Dick had told me she knew of a writing job at Scripps Aquarium (part of the campus). This sounded perfect. He had found out all the particulars, seemed to want me to pursue finding out about it. It sounded good to me, too. When I talked to Dodie, she said, "There are several excellent applicants. I'll do you a favor. I'll attach a cover letter of yours to the application. You can say in detail some of the things you've done. It might help. Give it to Dick to bring in tomorrow."

Then I met Dick and we walked to a little lunch area near his office. I told him about the letter. He asked, "Tonight? You're going to write it tonight?" I felt puzzled. I wondered why he questioned I could write it that night. "I'll have time," I said.

We shared a tunafish salad, and we walked around a little. His body was tense and rigid.

"What's wrong?" I said.

"I'm anxious. I have a lot of work to take care of. I should be back right now."

So we walked to my car.

We stood by the parking meter and he put his arms around me. I think I mumbled, "I love you," but I also worry that he asked, "Do you love me?" and that I might have said, "Yes," only in a half-caring way. But I really can't remember. I don't know if I am blocked, or if I just fear I didn't reassure him when he needed it the very most. I remember saying, "Well,

73

we'll have fun this Saturday." We had tickets to the San Diego Film Festival to see *Remember My Name*.

"I've even got someone lined up to stay with Richard that night," I said. It would have been the first time we had really been out for months. I was looking forward to it.

He walked away from me. It was a sunny, blue-sky day. He stopped and turned around about ten or twelve feet away from me. He was standing near a small tree. He just stood there, as if suspended in time, as if he didn't know whether to come toward me, or go from me, as if he were reluctant to leave.

I said, "What?" Then he said, "Oh, nothing." I started to sit in the car and I said to him as he turned to go, "Well, I don't know . . . we'll just do something—maybe watch TV tonight." Then he was gone. It was somewhere around two o'clock.

Later that day the mail brought news of a recipe contest I had won a small prize in. It was just a happy, fun message. It was around four. I called Dick just to share a little excitement I had. He said, "That's neat," or "That's good." We talked just a little bit. Then he said he had to go. He seemed a little rushed, and I felt he was busy, but otherwise it was not an unusual conversation.

An hour or so passed.

I fixed an eggplant casserole. Dick and I liked that, even if Richard didn't.

The casserole was cooking. I put out vegetables and dip. I poured a little glass of wine, and I expected him home any minute. He always drove up around five-thirty—by six if he stayed a little late, and then he would call. It's funny how attuned a person can be to the sound of a certain car. There is a personality to a particular hum of motor. I could always tell when he turned the corner, the way his emergency brake sounded, the slam of the door, the footsteps, the opening of the screen door, and then the feel of his arms around me.

But none of that happened.

I went back to my typewriter and decided to work on the letter for Dodie. I worked at it for a little while, then I walked back into the kitchen and looked out the door.

By six-thirty I was worried. "Richard," I said, "I'm a little worried. Dad should be home by now." Richard said, "Mom, nothing could have happened."

More time passed. I called his office, but there was no answer.

I tried to go back and work on the letter, but fear was rising inside me. This wasn't like Dick.

I called the highway patrol. I had done that once before in a time of panic, and Dick kidded me about it later. But I couldn't help it. I was beginning to be frightened and tearful. No accidents, they said.

I turned off the oven. I walked back and forth. Then I remembered I could call some of his coworkers. I called Dale, head of his department. I called Ed, who worked closely with Dick. They didn't know anything. Ed said to call back if he wasn't home soon.

Somewhere around eight or eight-thirty I called campus police. "Was his car in the parking lot by the library? Would you check his office to see if he could have passed out, or had some kind of attack? . . . No, he's never had an attack, but he must be hurt or unconscious somewhere. Otherwise he would be calling me and Richard to let us know he is OK." I believed this with all my heart. They said they would check and call me back.

"Richard," I said, half-jokingly, half-fearful—trying to make light of it, as terror rose in me and my palms grew damp and cold, "you don't suppose Dad got tired of us and just ran away from home, do you?"

I became more filled with panic. Unable to contain it, I called Larry, Dick's and my good friend. "Larry, I'm worried. Dick hasn't come home. Something is wrong." Larry had been asleep and he said, "Do you want me to come over?"

"No," I said, "I just had to talk to someone. I'm afraid."

"Call me again if you need me."

The next day Larry told me that he went back to sleep and dreamed a spaceship picked Dick up near the library on campus.

Sometime later I called Bonnie, my neighbor. I asked her if she could come and be with me, that Dick hadn't come home

75

and I was worried. Bonnie came, and it meant a lot to have her there. She fixed tea, and her presence was something to attach to.

Soon Richard said, "Mom, do you think it's OK for me to go to bed?" I said, "Sure, Richard," and as I tucked him in, I said, "Just go to sleep. Everything will be OK in the morning. You'll see. Don't worry. When you wake up, Dad will be here."

I wanted so much to believe that, but my panic wouldn't cease. I called my brother, Bud, and sister-in-law, Marcia, in Julian, sixty miles from here. I told them Dick hadn't come home, that something had to be wrong. Bud said they would come.

Around ten I heard a knock at the door. It was Dale, head of Dick's department at work, and his wife, Mary. Their faces looked cold and pale. They came in and sat down. Dale said, "The car is still in the parking lot—and they found a note addressed to you in it. Another note for Ed was on his desk."

Shock drained me. "No . . . What did it say?"

The words felt taut and hard, seared with pain.

Dale said simply, "That he would do harm to himself."

"No, oh, no. Oh, God, no. Please."

I felt horror-stricken. I could barely talk.

"Can I see it?"

"No," they said, "it's at the campus police station. We can drive you up there."

Bonnie stayed in the house with Richard.

At the campus police station I was shown the notes. Mine began, "Karen, This job has killed me." Then he went on to say Richard and I didn't do it, and that he had always loved us. And he said, "You know where my important papers are." It was just signed, "Dick," in very clear, slightly larger letters as if it were the last time he would write his name. Ed's letter spoke of frustration, of not being able to please everyone, of a feeling of failure. It was not signed.

I felt numb and unreal.

I thought he would go to the beach, because he loved the ocean. The police said they would "comb the campus," so I asked Mary and Dale to drive me to our favorite beach and then to the Ocean Beach pier. I thought he might have walked or hitchhiked to get there. The police told me to go home and

76

wait by the phone. They said many times the person threatening to kill himself will call after a while.

Dale and Mary drove me to the ocean. The sand and sea were dark, with only faint glimmers of the white foam reflecting pale moonlight. I called his name, but it seemed so futile to call someone's name over the sound of waves, into the vast darkness. No answer came.

We walked to the end of the pier—asked some boys if they had seen a man with dark hair on the pier.

No one had.

They drove me home, and inside Bonnie was still waiting.

"No," she said, "Dick hasn't called."

There is no way to describe the horror of such a night. The hours that go by—the unreality. You want to know what has happened, and yet you don't want to know. You have lost faith in God and goodness, and still you cling to God like a child. Earlier Richard and I had both knelt in prayer, something we'd never done before. "Please God—let Dick—let Dad—come home OK." But all the time sensing that prayer would not be answered as we wished.

Once I had a very strong feeling of Dick's presence in the living room, near the fireplace. But that time does not coincide with the time of his death. Was it my imagination? Was he thinking of me especially then?

Sometime around one or two in the morning Bud and Marcia came. After a while Bonnie left. I kept waiting for the phone to ring. Every once in a while I would call campus police. Still no trace of him. Yes, they had checked the cliff where hang gliders take off.

Soon it was daybreak. I had to wake Richard for school. I said, "Richard, you have to get up, but Richie, Dad still hasn't come home. I'm sorry. Do you want to go to school? If you get too worried there, you can come home."

"Yes," he said, "I want to go to school."

My brother drove him.

Bonnie's husband, Phil, called to say he had contacted the Coast Guard to start searching with helicopters now that it was daylight.

I called Missing Persons. Now that enough time had elapsed, they could start looking too.

As I was giving the report, four people from Dick's office came in. I just stood there with the phone in my hand, and then I put it down. I could see it in their faces. "I don't have to call Missing Persons, do I?"

I looked at Dale. He shook his head.

"Is he alive?"

And someone said quietly, "No."

The unreality rang in my ears with a deafening buzz. I felt a pressing into myself.

I heard myself say, "What happened? Where is he?"

"He jumped from a building."

This reality was not reality. Time expanded. There was nothing to do or say. I held my hands together and sat down. When I looked back at them they were still standing there just looking at me.

Fearful numbness filled my whole body, my voice, my ears, the room. "I don't believe it. It can't be." But I knew it must be so. And I tried to press the reality into my brain. This was not a time of crying out. This was a time of hanging on.

Richard called from school at about that time. My brother must have answered the phone. He went to the school to get Richard.

When Richard came in, I told him to come and sit down, and then I had to say the hardest words I've ever had to say.

I said, "Richard, Dad isn't coming home. Richard . . . Dad died." (That word was so hard to say, and it still is.) "Richard, it's just you and me now." He looked quickly down and said, "Did he do it to himself?"

I discovered later he had overheard when Dale and Mary told me about the note. Richard had been awake then and had worried too through the night.

We hugged each other. It was the end of the life the three of us had shared together, the life Richard had known all his years, and of what I had known for half my life.

> You fell into the air
> sailed for a moment,

78

a raven-haired bird.
I caught you with
        my heart.

(For Dick, November 15, 1978)

# 7 / Dick—Scenes

On a happy day, six months before Dick's death, amid subtle, lovely twilight colors at the beach, the Cove, in La Jolla, Dick, Richard, and I had just shared a picnic. The air was balmy—wonderful and soft like baby's breath. Dick and Richard began to play Frisbee. They were laughing and running and I turned my attention to the waves rolling in. A meditative mood came over me, and a poem came out of me that included the stanzas,

> "The sh . . . sh . . . sound
> of the ocean quiets us.
> It drinks us over and over."

*and*

> "Sh . . . be still
> and know
> things come
> and go."

(May 26, 1978)

It seems to me now that the poem was strangely prophetic, and that we were perhaps all held in a timeless moment when everything was known.

But that moment slips away, and I try to grasp . . . who was Dick? What was he like?

*Scene:* The ocean, waves washing on the shore—Richard and I are on the beach. Richard is perhaps five or six. Dick is in the water. Suddenly he comes rushing out, covered with seaweed. He runs toward Richard, arms outstretched, a look of mock ferocity on his face. He grabs Richard and runs with him, just into the smaller waves. They both come out laughing, and Richard is saying, "Dad, do it again." Dick, later, saying to me, "If I'm any kind of animal—I'm a sea otter."

*Scene:* The Catholic church in Lake Forest, Illinois. Dick is nine years old. He piously plays his role as altar boy. The candles flicker, the smell of incense fills him. He is somehow proud he has been chosen to do this task.

*Scene:* Quantico, Virginia, 1963. Dick being fitted for uniforms—khaki uniforms, fatigues, dress blues, dress whites, black gloves, white gloves, fatigue caps, khaki caps, dress blue cap, dress white cap, belts, insignia, shirts, ties, white shoes, black shoes, combat boots, rifle, engraved sword. Where is Dick in all this? Where, in this fancy game we are playing?

*Scene:* Mishawaka, Indiana, May 8, 1940. Dick is born, the oldest of three children. His father, a commercial artist, his mother, a housewife with an unused degree in economics. He is a beautiful baby, and both parents are proud of him.

*Scene:* The Cannery in San Francisco, a small print shop. Dick and I look through prints of Georgia O'Keeffe's series of posters done for the Santa Fe Chamber Music Festival—both of us trying to decide between the deep purple trumpet flowers, or the seashell—finally deciding on the seashell.

*Scene:* The green area in front of the Old Globe Theater, the summer before Dick's death. Dick and I are there with Richard and one of Richard's friends, to watch the "dancing on the green." I notice a man in the crowd, with a little girl on his shoulders. He looks like Tony, who was Dick's best man at our wedding—Tony whom we hadn't seen for fifteen years. He

81

stares at me, too—and then comes walking toward us. "Karen?" he says. "Tony! I can't believe it!" Then Dick turns around and looks almost shyly surprised. Tony looks the same as always—except for a very few gray hairs, almost as if a Hollywood makeup artist has only painted in a sprinkling of gray so that it will be believable that time has passed. Tony says he would have recognized me anywhere, but that Dick looks different—the beard and mustache, he says. Tony says he is in town for only a few days, from Atlanta, and didn't realize we lived in San Diego. He tells us he has four children.

*Scene:* Our last anniversary—February 14, 1978. Dick giving me an exquisitely carved wooden box. He found it in a nostalgia shop. It must have been caked with paint. Each night for weeks after dinner, he had gone into the garage to work on his secret project, cleaning the lacy wooden strips. Typical of the gifts he has given me, it represents beauty, care, and time.

*Scene:* Dick, coming home from scuba diving, two or three years before his death, saying to me, with concern in his green eyes, "Karen, I almost didn't make it—it was great doing the dive—beautiful, clear—the fish and undersea plants, but then when I came up, I couldn't find my partner, and I was in a riptide. I really panicked. I tried to just stay afloat on my back and move with the tide, and I just kept having to feel determined and not give up—it would have been easier to give up. I just didn't know if I would ever make it. When I finally washed up on the shore, I just lay there. . . ."

*Scene:* Dick, reading a short story by Kurt Vonnegut, Jr., entitled, "Unready to Wear," a story about people who drop their bodies anytime they want to, and choose others if they like. The story meant so much to Dick he shared it with at least two close friends.

*Scene:* Dick, talking on the phone—pacing, pacing—an intensity inside—something of a caged animal inside? Something under the surface he can't acknowledge?

*Scene:* University of New Mexico, Albuquerque, 1960. Dick and I help decorate the large Christmas tree in his fraternity house. His nickname in college is "Digger." He's never exactly understood why, and yet he accepts it as a personality someone has given him. He has just dropped his major of engineering.

82

Engineering feels somehow wrong, he tells me. "I'm switching to business," he says, "it's too late to switch to anything else."

*Scene:* One year before his death. Leaving the movie theater after seeing *Coming Home*, a movie about Vietnam veterans— discussing whether or not Bruce Dern, the actor who played the Marine officer and Jane Fonda's husband, really committed suicide at the end. Dick and I both say Yes, he did. Mary, who went with us, being optimistic, says Maybe he didn't really.

*Scene:* Dick is two years old. His parents worry. He has never spoken, and yet he seems bright. Then one night they hear a voice coming from Dick's and his baby brother's room. Dick is talking, trying to teach his baby brother to talk. "See, Tommy, this is your bear . . . can you say 'bear,' Tommy?"

*Scene:* The beach, La Jolla, a dress picnic with friends—china plates and wine glasses. Dick wears the most outrageous outfit, carries his Marine Corps sword, wears a large decorated hat given him on his last birthday by fun-loving friends. Everyone thinks he is very funny—more daring in that way than anyone else—more willing to play the fool—that he has a wonderful sense of humor.

*Scene:* Dick, waking up extra early every morning, three or four years before his death, so that he can read a chapter or two from Jacob Bronowski's *The Ascent of Man*, Carl Sagan's *The Dragons of Eden*, or Loren Eiseley's *The Immense Journey*.

*Scene:* An old photo—Dick is dressed in a mannish-looking hat and overcoat. He is about twelve or thirteen years old, and a strikingly beautiful young boy. He is president of his eighth grade class.

*Scene:* Dick's dark head bent, his large eyes gazing on his firstborn, his son, Richard, as he holds him delicately for the first time.

*Scene:* Dick, at an opening of a juried art show where his second piece of stained glass was chosen to hang. Dick, almost shyly eyeing his own work, wondering how people will see it— wondering out loud to me if it is really good enough to hang there with the other fine works. His own work, entitled, ". . . and a space"—the green, purple, and pale yellow pieces forming an oval, almost a floral shape. One area kept free of glass, and that, he said, was the most important area—the space.

*Scene:* Dick, playing basketball in college—falling and breaking his wrist—saying he was glad I didn't come to that game—that I would have gotten upset.

*Scene:* The Civic Theater, San Diego, our seats in the fifth row. Chuck Mangione's music fills the theater and our spirits—and Dick's hand reaches over to take mine.

*Scene:* Quantico, Virginia, 1963, coming home from the "three-day war," the practice war in basic training—grimy, tired, determined—almost a small satisfied look under the tired surface—Dick expresses a feeling of adequacy that he has made it—completed all the tasks and maneuvers as he was supposed to. Later, after showering, falling asleep with me on the couch, the TV on, our arms wrapped around each other.

*Scene:* Dick, sitting on the couch, feeding Johanna—always a touched, tender look on his face when he held her or looked on her.

*Scene:* Dick's tall, slim form standing in the Little League bleachers—his arms raised to cheer Richard on, as Richard runs around the bases: "Come on Richard—come on—you're almost there!"

*Scene:* Ensenada, Mexico. We are at the "blow-hole" south of town. Intermittently the ocean rushes into a deep crevice in the cliff, and the resultant intense force spews the water dramatically into the air—100 feet or so. Dick climbing down the side of the crevice, down near the source of the energy—an area now off limits because of its danger.

*Scene:* An NROTC dance, during college days at UNM, probably 1960. Dick and I pass under the awning of raised, crossed swords—and we kiss. It is a pageant of sorts—when the whistle blows, you stop kissing and another couple begin to pass under the swords. We kiss for a long time—then Dick's friend, in charge of the whistle-blowing, says, grinning, "I just couldn't blow the whistle on you guys."

*Scene:* Summer before his death—Dick marching in a parade downtown, from the Civic Theater to the Embarcadero, to protest the harboring here for two days of the *Esmerelda*, the Chilean torture ship. He felt that in the name of humanity we

84

shouldn't allow it to dock here—that it was important to make a stand.

*Scene:* Dick, in the recent past, coming back from an early morning tennis game, looking muscular and fit—annoyed that he didn't play as well as he wanted to that day, somehow angry at himself.

*Scene:* Dick, going night scuba diving. Me, going along, then feeling fearful watching him walk out into the black, black sea—waiting, wondering how long before he comes back. Later he tells me how beautiful it was, how as the fish were held in the circle of light beamed by his underwater flashlight, they all seemed slower, almost transfixed in the night sea.

I always felt we were very close, that we were somehow bound up together, that the circle we lived in enclosed all our experience—times when we loved and times when we were distant.

Now of course I know very well that even those we feel closest to have secret parts, unknown to us. No one ever really knows another. Few of us ever really even know ourselves. But the illusion persists.

I found some writings of Dick's, almost a year after he died. These words were written in a class he was in (1974, four years before his death), and in response to certain concepts, but they speak directly for him and from him.

*Contentment.* If I were completely content with everything, I wouldn't be here probably (in class). I wouldn't need to make the effort. However I'm in a questioning stage of my life right now, specifically in terms of career job desires. My present position in Personnel is certainly demanding, it pays well, and seems fairly secure. However, I'm not really using myself to the utmost, by any means. I feel I really have more to contribute. Where this will lead to I don't know. I know I'm having some problem regarding security and not really being ready to rock the boat and take a risk, possibly take a big immediate pay cut to go into some new field. But soon, some big step is going to be taken or else I'll explode!!

85

*Experiential Transcendence.* This refers to one of the methods we can employ to achieve some type of "symbolic immortality." Under this method, the resultant altered states of consciousness are so strong and so important to us that such things as time and death are almost forgotten. The closest I can get to this would be the way I feel when I'm scuba diving. I feel so much in a "separate place" and so *alive,* that other thoughts, other problems are nonexistent, or at least unimportant.

*Personal Integration.* I will say that I do, at least guardedly, feel like myself while moving through my roles. In order to do it I often have to shut (out) a certain amount, at least of all of the answers to life that the media provides. It's not easy, and does require some kind of transcendence. So I dive. It allows the other roles to be handled.

And then, four years later, he had written in his last communication, "For some reason my rope ran out after only 38 years worth of use. Why? I don't know. I just don't know at all . . ."

Dick was that father playing on the beach with his son, full of enthusiasm and joy—"Come on, Richard"—teasing and playful, energetic. And he was my friend, my lover, procreator of our children, sharer of my joys and sorrow, my excitement and my searchings, and he is all the things I observed about him, that others observed about him and felt for him, but I guess I can't say what he was to himself, really, and that is what he truly was, of course. All else is only reflection. Who he was to himself is his alone, and there is something precious, unknown, and almost holy about that.

> The bird
> does not fall
> The line of pelicans
>      goes on forever
>
> The colors of morning
> rise

over and over
You drank them like the air.

The bird
spreads its wings,
flies
into seas of color,
swoops low
for a moment,
then
lifts
into waiting clouds.

(For Dick November 23, 1978)

# 8 / Passage

We never talked of death,
not as if it would happen to us really.

We weren't prepared for it,
but you secretly made your plans.

We never talked of death.
Of all the things we talked about
and never did,
You did the one thing
we never really did discuss.

I guess you began to think
talk is cheap.

(September 30, 1979)

One of the things that hurt the most is that no time existed
to tie up any loose ends, no time to cherish the last moment of

88

life, no time to say all I would have wanted to say, no time to say all the I love yous, all the I'm sorrys (that you're going, that life hurt you, that I didn't understand, or love you enough, or the right way . . . that you didn't destroy your job, rather than yourself, that we didn't move or start over), no time to show tenderness often held back. No time to just say—Hey, it was nice, I'm glad we shared a lot of life together. No time to say any of the things that make up goodbye. I wished he had just gotten on a train, run away, left our life. I even wished he had beaten me up. Now I had to try to swallow my guilts, hang fast to my love, believe in what we had had, and trust him—alone. I had felt he was the best friend I'd ever had. Now I questioned if I had been his. There would be no growing old together (something incomprehensible to me at first), no more sharing of each day together, or of each other, no more his arms around me, his body almost a part of me, no more babies, no more trips to San Francisco together, no more music to enjoy together, no more shared joys, or sorrows, no more hope for us.

One day life was normal. I heard my husband's voice on the phone during the day, the car drove up each night as I was fixing dinner, he lay beside me each night in bed. Suddenly it had ended without a clear warning that I could discern, as if it had all been a dream.

That morning after Dick's coworkers told me the news, after I had to tell Richard his father was no longer alive, I then had to call Dick's parents. It was hard to talk, hard to say the words. Those words didn't seem real. How can you tell someone the life they brought into the world just gave it back?

Dick's father, also named Dick, said simply, "I can't believe that. I don't know what to say. I can't believe Rick would do that."

He told me Chris, Dick's mother, had gone for a walk on the beach, and that he would find her and tell her.

Later she called, had been crying, and we talked of the arrangements for them to come. There was a strange rationality about making the plans—a kind of insanity in the structure and order in relation to the shock, horror, and disbelief.

Other calls I could not make. My sister-in-law, Marcia, made a lot of them, and then friends called other friends.

I had to call the mortuary—the first day I suppose, though I don't recall specifically. I told them what Dick had always said to me—that he wished to be cremated and have his ashes sprinkled in the ocean. Some people have questioned how I could have done this. All I know is that it is what Dick wanted and I wanted to honor his wishes. Though I was at the time unfamiliar with Eastern beliefs regarding cremation, I have now recently read the Eastern belief is that it is necessary to burn the body in order to liberate the soul and that the fire represents the sun or god action or transmutation; that the body is of no real consequence in a soul's journey and development except as a vehicle to be used temporarily and discarded like old clothing at death. I rather like that explanation, and I feel certain those must have been Dick's feelings. How absurd it is to worry about our bodies. If anything persists, it is the spirit.

At one point though I felt I should go to see Dick's body, but the mortician said, "It's often best to remember someone as that person was. It doesn't make a good last memory to see someone's body, especially if that person was injured."

I accepted what he said, for I felt fearful of that encounter. I was terrified of going alone, and I felt there was no one to go with me and support me. I called Dick's mother. She felt the same way. She said she remembered him as a baby and a child. That was enough. It was easy for me to agree. So no one, none of his family, saw Dick once he was no longer alive.

The coroner came with a little envelope of Dick's belongings—his wedding ring, his wallet with forty-two cents in it, and his diving watch, still running. Dick hadn't worn his wedding ring much lately, so it seemed ironic he had it on when he died. He and I both had gone through a period when we didn't always wear our rings—feeling that a ring was only an outward symbol of the tie between us. Somewhere in the last couple of years I had gone back to wearing my wedding band, but Dick hadn't felt a need to do that. He had lately worn a handcrafted silver ring with malachite set in it instead. One morning, only a few weeks before Dick's death, Richard came into our bedroom, picked up Dick's hand, and said, "Why aren't you wearing your wedding ring?" Richard took the ring from the top of the dresser and put it on Dick's finger. The fact that he had only forty-two cents in his pocket was typical. He seldom carried money. He was not attached to material possessions and didn't seek that sort of security.

I felt drugged. My body was heavy. My mind couldn't think. I felt I could barely talk. I sat on the couch for two days, only lying down on it that first night to sleep (with a sleeping pill). I didn't take my clothes off. I felt I couldn't change anything—didn't want to move my body, change clothes, or eat. This was part of unreality and of hanging on, I guess. That feeling persisted for many months afterwards, though in a reduced way.

My fingernails grew for the first time, even the one on my wedding ring finger that I always bit, and I didn't get my hair trimmed for at least seven or eight months—something I always did every six weeks or so. I felt somehow wrong about having anything cut off.


The first couple of days blended. Friends started to come to the house. They brought food and just sat with me. Richard was out riding his bike, and was with friends in the neighborhood much of the time—seldom was he in the house.

Dick's parents and his brother, Tom, were here within a day or two, and the next day the memorial service was held. I chose a place by the ocean in La Jolla, a grassy space above the sand. I remember it was sunny and I wore an orchid blouse and skirt Dick had liked. I bought pinkish-purple carnations to take along.

Sixty or seventy people came. They stood in a circle, while a minister we had known for years spoke for a few minutes, then read this poem of mine. Dick had always liked it:

> The surfer,
> like the twilight sea
> struggles to push out past rippling waves,
> breaking gently on the breathing sand.

91

Alert eyes look
to the horizon
and yearn to join other black seal-men
waiting in line for their wave.

He pushes and struggles,
paddles his sea arms frantically,
kicks his black legs and bare white feet,
as the ocean sucks away, away,
as if it is holding its breath.

And then just as he reaches
the others,
it begins to swell forward and break,
all across the pearl-turquoise sea,
and beneath the luminous pink bird-feather sky,
the wave comes
as if it had waited
just for him.

(originally written January 3, 1978;
first line slightly revised
November 6, 1978, and dedicated to Dick)

Then I had asked the minister to read these lines from Dylan
Thomas' poem, "And Death Shall Have No Dominion":

And death shall have no dominion. . . .
With the man in the wind and the west moon; . . .
They shall have stars at elbow and foot; . . .
Though they sink through the sea they shall rise again;
Though lovers be lost   love shall not;
And death shall have no dominion.

He then said The Lord's Prayer. And Al, our friend, played
the same Spanish lullaby on his guitar that he had played at
Johanna's ceremony. When the notes ended, everyone, one by
one, came to me—all the faces from our life together here in
San Diego, some I hadn't seen for years. When someone is

about to die they say life passes before his or her eyes. I felt in a sense that was happening to me, as each person Dick and I had spent time with, shared some of our life together with, came toward me.

When most of our friends were gone I took the carnations and threw them each separately into the sea.

Richard didn't seem affected by the service. In fact, in his twelve-year-old mind, deeply shocked, I don't think it seemed quite real to him. He was in this state for quite a while before the reality finally was part of his life.

Chris and Dick, Dick's parents, told me later it meant a lot to them to see all of Dick's friends together at the service. This somehow gave them comfort and I guess helped validate for them the person he had been, the person they hadn't seen much the last few years.

I wrote one entry in my journal, November 6, 1978, in very small handwriting:

What I would never have believed could happen has happened. I can barely write it. Dick is no longer here. He has died. He is gone. He took his own life. Half of my life is gone.

Perhaps it was the next day when I called the Old Mission here in San Diego. The priest agreed to offer a mass for Dick that evening. Dick's parents, Richard, and I all attended. Later the priest came over. Chris told him that the death was due to suicide. The young priest said simply, "The church now takes pity on those who can't help themselves."

In a few days my brother and I, along with Dick's parents, took the box of ashes and went out to sea in a boat owned by a friend Dick had often gone diving with. Two other friends came down to the landing to see us off—to say a last earthly goodbye to Dick's remains. The boat took off in a surge of power.

Only one boat passed us, crisply cutting and shattering the water, heading back out to sea. Her name was *Faith*.

Once far enough off shore, and directly in line with the grassy spot where we had held the service, the boat engine was shut down. The boat gently rocked on the waves as my brother cut open the box and I took it from him. I leaned over the side and shook Dick's ashes into the water, and then I cried as the motor churned again and we took off. I felt at one with the force of the foaming water gushing and lashing after us like the ferocious giant white tail of a dragon, like a liquid scream. Chris and Dick sat huddled together, their faces tight, their eyes cast down.

We had buried him. No one who has done this can ever say that you don't feel the touch of dreadful mortality, and yet I believe now it is only one reality.

Georgia O'Keeffe painted roses alongside cow skulls. Two shapes that happen to complement each other. One is not seen as ugly, and the other as beautiful. Both are shapes, forms that exist in relation to each other. The connotations of life and nonlife seem to cease as they are captured in those moments of existence.

Chris and Dick went back to Florida. Tom flew home to Illinois. My brother, Bud, and Marcia went back to their life in Julian, and Richard and I began to learn how to go on.

# 9 / The Questions

*Brushstrokes (Why?)*

The finishing touches, or brushstrokes, on Dick's life were and are filled in by those who knew him, and by those who didn't know him and only know of his act.

They say the test of greatness in literature is how much criticism and interpretation is written about a work. It is true that any work of art speaks to many in a variety of ways.

Like Picasso's statue in Daley Square, in Chicago, Dick's suicide brings forth the full range of emotion. Some feel they understand it, some hate it, some accept it, some condemn it, some don't even want to see it, but its presence stays and won't be denied.

It seems to me Dick's act can be seen in the same light as such a rather controversial and abstract work. It was a statement. It exists forever as it was executed, and then the viewers come to interpret, to cover over, to confuse, to soften, to sharpen, to try to make clear. Everyone views any statement or work of art

95

through his or her own screen of reality. It's all relative. Our perception is only ours, and we are all only truly seeing for brief moments or flashes in our lives. As Willem de Kooning, the abstract painter, has said, "We are all 'slipping glimpsers.'"

The views of Dick's suicide were many and varied:

"He was a martyr, maybe like Jesus. He was definitely trying to make a statement."

"He did it on campus, not at home, and so he hated the campus."

"He wouldn't have wanted you to find him. He was protecting you."

"He was an angry man."

"He was not an angry man. It was an act of despair."

"He was too good."

"He was totally out of touch with reality."

"He was not mentally ill. It was a logical choice he made."

"How do you know it wasn't best for him? Not best for you, but best for Dick?"

"He should have had medication."

"He wouldn't have done that. I just can't believe he would have done that."

"Some say childhood causes these things, but I think it has to do with chemical imbalance."

"It was definitely a chemical imbalance. He was losing weight."

"It didn't fit his psychological make-up."

"It was his job—all the pressure."

"It wasn't his job. It was that he was ill."

"It was just a choice he made."

"I feel so angry at Dick's act—it is why I haven't written you."

"He turned against you. Can't you see that? Can't you feel his rejection of you?"

"He did it for you."

Or as one friend said, "Perhaps it was a part of Dick that was like one of the moons of Saturn—always there—but no one knew about it—and it was unknown even to Dick."

The question "Why?" plays on our deepest fear, our deepest guilt, self-doubt, and sense of failure, our fear of loss of

96

control, of others, of ourselves. I couldn't keep him from doing it, and he couldn't keep himself from doing it. But the line is thin. Perhaps for Dick it was total control. They look the same. The result was the same.

Was it for no reason, or was it for all the reasons, or was it for no apparent reason? Why that choice? The truth is we don't really know, though we can conjecture. The existence of the fact and the acceptance of the unknowingness, is perhaps all. That is the "faith," the "faith" written on the side of the boat as it passed us on his last trip out to sea.

All the words are only attempts to make clear, and still the true clearness exists only in the acknowledgement.

In my heart only one reality exists. He is no longer here, and I am still alive. There don't have to be "reasons" for anything anymore. It's that simple. It's that complex.

The painting remains there like a question, and it alone gives the answer.

Pablo Picasso

## The Right to Die—The Right to Live (Why Not?)

In time the questions begin to still and the mystery is accepted, like rough water that eventually settles. Perhaps the most awesome gift we can be given in life is a mystery.

Like an intricate Chinese box, there are smaller boxes inside, and yet it keeps unfolding like a flower.

Part of the puzzle is the question, "Do we have the right to die?" If we feel too much pain, mental or physical, then that peaceful rest might seem appealing, but do we have the right to choose it? Though it is hard for me to separate Dick's right to die from my hurt and loss, and especially from Richard's hurt and loss, maybe that is the only obstacle in the way. While I wish he had chosen options, I have to honor his decision.

I am pained and saddened to think of the mental suffering he must have gone through. And yet, in his state of mind, in his reality, it must have seemed the perfect thing to do. He didn't do what I wanted him to do, what Richard wanted him to do. This was not his parents' choice, his coworkers' or his friends' choice. This final choice was made totally alone. It was Dick's choice. He labored through the night, and he gave birth to his death.

He must have wanted release, and I guess he has that now, though I wish he hadn't had to do it. The ultimate question, after all, isn't "Did he have the right to do it?" but is perhaps "Why should he have had to do it?"

On the other hand, when someone is left as I was, there is the opposite question, "Do I have the right to live?" I have struggled not with taking my life, in the sense of losing it, but with taking my life, using it, and feeling I have a right to live, in the fullest sense.

Maybe that is the hardest hurdle for survivors. There is grief. There is loss. But are we ever absolved? My thoughts for a long time questioned if I deserved to live.

Journal excerpt, December 4, 1979:
The hardest thing, and it's getting better, is to believe that I deserve this new life. It's here for the taking—the sun, the sea, my friends, my son, art, music, touching some-one's hand.

I know my old self died. I know my new self is infinitely wiser, though far from wise. . . . Do I deserve to be loved is not the essential question. The essential question is, do I deserve to love?

And even if I don't deserve to—shouldn't I anyway? The question of to be or not—is really to love or die. If we live, then we must love. If we love, we live. They are insepara-ble.

Now piece by piece I am trying to take back my right to life, trying to learn to live for myself, for Richard, and with friends, and new people in my life.

Now for the first time in my life I'm beginning to truly know myself alone, and to be able, then, to share that self here and there with others, and to have a beginning sense of purpose.

Deserving to live is much more than survival.

There are no ends to the intricate boxes, the questions. The more I think I know or understand, the less I truly know, and yet each question opens another door.

I have been given the supreme puzzle of life. I can either spend my life analyzing it, or I can accept it as a key to life:

| | |
|---|---|
| We can never have control | (We have to surrender, and that is our choice and our control.) |
| We can never have security | (Things come and go. We can depend on that with security.) |
| We can never own love | (Love exists, and we gain it by not possessing it.) |
| We can never understand | (We have to accept, and that is understanding.) |

The puzzles rise over and over, but the clues given have little to do with the past and everything to do with the present and future.

## What About the Gentle Men?

Where can they go,
the gentle men,
when the wars rage on
and the storms press down?
When the stars fall down?
Where do they hide?

How do they go,
the gentle men,
when no one will hear
and hands are cold,
when eyes are not clear,
when the space is too wide?
How can they be?

Must they then leave,
the gentle men,
if trees are leafless
and houses seem shells?

Do their hearts seal over?
Do their spirits fall like rain?
Where can they live?

(June 10, 1980)

How does a gentle man survive? In Dick's case, he doesn't, except in our hearts, and on these pages. His tragedy, I think, is the tragedy of that gentle side of all men—larger in some, barely noticeable in others. His tragedy was perhaps that of being too sensitive, feeling too much of the pain of the world while not acknowledging enough of his own pain, his own needs, and the tragedy of being locked into a job which gave him no real creative outlet. When he tried to bring his human values into it, those values were dismissed. Unseeing eyes denied them over and over again. And his was perhaps also the tragedy of not being seen by me, or others, as he truly was, and of not being able to show himself as he was, and of letting feelings of failure gnaw away at his sense of worth.

But the need to persevere was perhaps the tragic flaw, the tragedy of insisting upon enduring, never crying for help. Dick could stick with something and concentrate intensely on it. He was utterly lacking in self-indulgence. He didn't feel, as most people do, that his desires were of utmost importance. He had a strong nurturing side, but this nurturing did not extend to himself.

As James Kavanaugh has said in one of his poems, "There are men too gentle to live among wolves."

How can a gentle man survive with his fragility? Does survival for a gentle man mean he has to lead a schizophrenic existence? Must he learn to hide and protect that vulnerable and loving part, to keep it separate from the world that bombards with demands for conformance to its rules, for an

100

outer show of success, for what it terms achievement—and which denies the tears and tenderness of a man?

Are the gentle men the truest victims of our patriarchal society? A society that requires performance, a product, competitiveness, but considers the gentle side, the nurturing side second class?

As a result of upbringing, society, and perhaps inborn character traits, Dick had a highly developed sense of competition, expected outstanding performance from himself. At the same time he was imprisoned in an extremely sensitive nature that could not bear the resultant pain when he felt he did not live up to those self-imposed standards.

Perhaps when the gentle side of him was irrevocably beaten down in the university system in which he had tried to arbitrate his conflicting feelings for eight years, there was little left—of him. The final aggression at last was taken out on himself, because he felt so powerless to take it out anywhere else. He had tried, and over and over again he was suppressed until only a wafer-thin part of him was left—a crescent moon soon to slip into darkness—his soul a communion wafer he offered to the sunrise that morning.

I think it was an act of despair, born of negation, negation of self—the feeling of powerlessness that grew out of the stands he made which were not supported—the constant thwarting by the university system of his human values and decisions—this coupled with the feeling of psychological impotence he perhaps experienced because of the last miscarriage I had. These elements must have finally dealt the fatal blow. Everything knit together in a fatal knot—his character traits in that setting, coupled with the miscarriage and perhaps my absorption with the pregnancy and my misunderstanding of his withdrawal, perhaps gathered in a total loss of self-esteem.

He could muster strength from nowhere to live—only persevere to die—only try to take the darkness that surrounded him and finally become it—in order to find light.

He took a leap of faith. Everything was pushed to a point of no return—the unexpressed, the dreams unknown even to him, the childhood memories he could never recall, the subconscious he always seemed to have little access to, finally claimed him.

If the world had allowed his creativity, had accepted his love, if the standards society imposes on men were softer, if he could have not felt he needed to always live up to the "good boy" image and the challenge of "duty"—could he have lived?

How many men, and women too, I wonder, are trying to be successes, feeling great responsibility, unable to voice their own pain and frustration, or love? And even when they do—who of us allows their anger or their tears?

Was it easier for him to kill himself than to come home and say he just couldn't make it anymore?

Can men learn we are all interdependent—to be able to involve others in their pain—to be able to say—I need your help—to give the gift of needing help, the gift of involving another in the process of growth and struggle? To trust? Can women learn to let men be human and vulnerable—to see beyond the mask and the illusion and our own needs?

The fear for Dick and for many men maybe is that help will not be there, only exposure and humiliation. Society has told them to be a particular way—successful, achieving, aggressive—and they will be rewarded and accepted. As parents we nurture this in little boys; and as wives, brought up to expect it, we further the damning indictment.

The fear is justified. Acceptance may not always be there—but we have to begin to open the door. Until we set men free—until we, as men and women, set what is termed "feminine" in men free—there will be no real freedom, and the male dominance will destroy what is truly good, the gentleness, the searching, and expect the implied good—being responsible and strong.

# 10 / Death of Illusion—
## End of the Myth

We are fed fairy tales from infancy on—myths and folk tales have always been with us, whether they are present-day media myths or the often-told tales in children's books. We remember the happy endings. We notice the ads on TV and the happily-ever-afters more than the dragons and wicked witches. We remember that Cinderella became a princess for a night. We think her story ended when the tale was over, but there is always more—more dark and more light.

Maybe the false myths of happily-ever-after can destroy us, for they are only romantic tales. Maybe the true myths of struggle could save us, by helping us accept the true work of loving and by helping us find real wholeness through the meeting of the opposites of dark and light.

We believe that if our parents' lives were in conflict, ours will effortlessly be full of amity. We believe inside that we deserve to have what we want, but when this is denied us, then we also believe we probably deserved that denial even more, because

103

deep inside we never believed those happy endings were really meant for us anyway.

The romantic myth I grew up to believe said I should marry someone "good enough" for me—whatever that meant—and have children. I should be taken care of. I was sent to college "to meet someone," not to be someone.

After marriage I felt I was supposed to have babies, or be able to explain why to parents and to society. This was not so much said as just understood, sensed by me and others of my generation. The other part of this myth is that deep inside I believed in a protector. I believed and wanted someone to come to lift me from the turmoil of my home life, to love me, and at the same time, to not cut me off completely from my past. Dick was that person. He offered love, protection. He cherished me, appreciated me. He had the qualities I cared for, and I loved him. He did not deny or cut me from my roots, while at the same time taking me physically away from them. All the parts of my life could come together in him in spirit.

If, as in the Greek myths, I was part Psyche (as the legend goes, born from a dewdrop, the gentle side of woman) I was also part Aphrodite (the stronger woman, conceived in the sea, borne to the land on a sea wave). Dick loved the Psyche part of me, the ephemeral side, and he was lover to that part of me. I think that when the Aphrodite in me surfaced, this part seemed to need less, or something other, and he could never respond to that part of me. Perhaps if a deeper, nurturing side of me had evolved, perhaps some new working relationship would have been born between us.

And Dick, what was this outer myth the world had planted in his mind? That he should be strong, in spite of the fact he was very gentle? That he should "take care of" in spite of the fact he probably wanted also to be "taken care of"—that he should sacrifice his life, before he really formed what he wanted to do with it, for the American dream of a wife, two children, a car, and a house? Why was the myth of provider uppermost in his mind? Why did so much of his feeling of worth come from that?

And maybe Dick, on his own quest, as all men are, for his

"Holy Grail," his own sense of perfection, loved me on his path as one of the reflections inside himself, as part of the feminine inside himself, on the way to that perfection. Was I, as a part of him, the woman who seduced him, the woman who psychologically supported him, and also the woman whom in many ways he couldn't touch? Was he finally able to drink from the grail in completion, in wholeness, alone that night?

Are we ever ourselves, or only parts in each other's personal myths and passion plays?

Did Dick and I fall into each other's traps—fulfill for each other the opposite half of fated coins? Though we came together in some strong, good ways, we also came together as many people do to fulfill unmet needs within ourselves. If we had both been unable to fulfill those neurotic needs through each other, would he still be alive? Or would we have kept seeking the fulfillment of those needs until we finally satisfied them? What does it take for us to learn and change and grow? I think it takes coming to that point, as the Orientals say, of "dangerous possibility,"—recognizing it, and then consciously choosing our direction, rather than subconsciously using one another. At this point there is either a symbolic death or rebirth.

If we listened more to the ancient myths of struggle, of choice, of consequence, where there are deep psychological truths, and less to the surface media myths of today that speak of deliverance, of happily-ever-after, that promise perfection and cause us to hide and feel shame for our flaws, could he have survived? Could we both, the early Dick and Karen, full of promise and hope, have survived and grown?

The ancient marriage rituals were a combination of celebration and sacrifice. Maybe if we could have more totally accepted the little sacrifices of everyday life we wouldn't have been so destined for the big one at the end. I wonder?

If all of us could know that every marriage is a marriage of light and shadow, and the beginning of a quest, not the ending of a quest—would we end up destroying each other so much? Maybe trust is the only solution—to have had true "faith" in one another, and in the order of the universe. It seems so

105

simple and almost trite to say it—but if we could see the other person, our mate, as a person, and not as a character fulfilling a role, wouldn't that then be the closest to freedom and love we'll ever know? And wouldn't that be deliverance and happily-ever-after?

As the saying goes, "Only love is real. Everything else is illusion."

# EARTH

Yellow
pushing through and growing

Do you deserve to be there?

Ashes
driftsticks
belong here.

Why are you daring
   and believing that you can,
   believing that you are?

# 11 / Grief Work

Having a death
is like having a baby,

Only it takes longer
to really be free.

It grows inside you,
and you work so hard
to push it clean
         away
            from you,
so that it is separate.

You still care,
it is still yours,
but it doesn't,
      can't
      live inside you,
      can't feed off of you forever.

(March 15, 1979)

In a sense a special kind of grief is the theme of this book, and grief is in some ways the theme of life. It is the process of letting go, and the process of letting go is the story of becoming.

There is an element of birth in this sense, connected with grief. Just as giving birth is letting go, letting go is giving birth. When a woman is pregnant she is given extra attention, and yet a person experiencing grief also needs care. Death takes its toll, even more than new life.

There are so many stages to grief, different for each person. Each stage has its own magic healing powers. Grief is a present, a tool, a passage.

It has been said it is an emotional response to an amputation of a part of a person's life.

Those experiencing grief are psychologically wounded, often filled with a sense of hopelessness and despair. Everything seems to bloom with pain and grayness, and yet every glint of sunshine is unexpected and beautiful and fleeting.

The beginning stages of grief seemed to me to be as heavy and gray as battleships, heavy as dark curtains, and yet those curtains did very gradually lift.

Journal excerpt, August 16, 1979:
There seem to be two phases, major phases, so far, for me. The first was the almost prenatal stage, the curling up in bed with Dick's ring on a chain around my neck, as I clutched it like a rosary—the seeking of comfort—those were the first few weeks. Now nine months later the world is opening more for me. It is in many ways more difficult. The shock is still there, the unreality, and mixed in now is an increase in questioning. I haven't accepted it—the fact—or not knowing the reason—or that I must go on. Layered on this is now the reality of life decisions. . . .

Every place I went for a long time reminded me of Dick, whether I had been with him in that place or not. The old places were haunted by him, but the new places too were expectant with "What would he think of this?" or "Would he like that?"

Stores cried out with shirts he would like, records he might

110

want, books he would have read, even presents he would have given me.

A friend of mine, Stefanie Ramsdell, wrote simply one day, capturing a facet of grief:

> You went suddenly
> Left my hands brimming with gifts—
> Nowhere to bring them.

All the "unfinished business" as Elizabeth Kubler-Ross has said, must be finished. The words unsaid, the gifts never given, are like threads in a tapestry that must be rewoven.

I thought constantly of all I hadn't said. I wanted to say, "I just didn't know . . ." but of course the words I wanted most to say—the essential message in life—is "I love you."

Grief is the price we pay for that love—said or unsaid, and it is the ship that eventually carries us through the passage of separation.

## Shock

In the beginning, grief took the form of shock. It covered me with an ability to go on. It looked like courage—maybe—but it is something that protects against the unacceptable and anesthetizes.

I did many things while in that initial state of shock. Besides planning the memorial service, in a week I made a little pamphlet with a picture of Dick to give to friends. In it I told them what happened, and what he was like. It was a tribute to him, so that people would remember and know him, and it helped my feelings have a place to go. I could express love for Dick in those words—love I had no other way to express.

Every night I sat at the kitchen table with bills I'd never paid before, trying to figure out finances—something I'd never wanted to know—and finding an unusual pleasure in their dependability and lack of emotion. I made lists of tasks. Rote thinking worked best. It held back the fear and terror.

I tried to create an order to life. I was working then from nine in the morning until one. Never mind that I often cried in the car, driving to and fro, or that I at least once screamed at the top of my lungs in that car. I would come home, pick up Richard at 2:15 after school, and we'd run errands, or do anything to be out of the house. In the state of shock, life is shot apart and makes no sense, until gradually a new sense comes. Dinnertime was a difficult part of the day. Sometimes we were lucky enough to be with people. Most often we weren't. Many times we would go to restaurants or cafes. Sometimes at night I'd build fires and try to warm myself, and I looked forward most of all to the time when I could go to sleep. To be blotted out was the best part of the day.

But the feeling of horror would break through unannounced, all over my body, like a cold chill—terror—disbelief. This happened less frequently with time, but happens sometimes, still.

I carried on a kind of constant conversation about Dick, with anyone I was with at the time. This too was part of the shock reaction—the constant retelling, in order to grasp, in order to make real what did not seem real, and in order not to let go of him.

Often when I saw people on the street, I thought how extraordinary that they like themselves enough to want to be alive—and Dick didn't—and then the feeling of incredibility would wash over me.

At certain times the feeling of immediate shock was renewed, such as when I first visited the actual place where he died. I felt a need, an urging to go there. I had thought I would want to sit nearby, maybe even lay a flower there. I asked Dick's coworker, Ed, if he would show me where it happened. He said, "OK. But on a sunny day." So one sunny day we walked across campus, past students playing tennis— bright green balls bouncing in the sun. When we came to the actual place of Dick's death I felt some coldness, but nothing else. I didn't feel I wanted to stay there, or leave flowers, or come back. I felt strongly I wanted to be away from there. That night after falling asleep I suddenly awakened and leaped out of bed, totally disoriented. For a few minutes, maybe only seconds, I didn't know who or where I was. This I realized later was a shock reaction.

112

One day I "accidentally" read a letter from the coroner which was in with some other papers. I read that there were no drugs of any kind in Dick's body—and he had no illnesses—"a healthy male Caucasian." This was as I expected. My hands flew to my mouth though when my eyes saw the words describing his injuries, and yet I had already read too much before I looked away, and this frightened me.

I don't know what the answer to shock is. Men who've gone to war can suffer from it all their lives. Doctors and nurses must live with the feeling every day, yet they still go on and rise above painful images that are in their minds.

Journal excerpt, February, 1980:
There is no way to describe it—the shock and horror I did feel and still sometimes feel. To have everything end so suddenly, so violently, and to know Dick was capable of it, that he did it, that I thought I knew him, that I thought he was stable, dependable—turns my world completely up-side down.
What can I believe in?
Can I trust my judgment?
How can I ever trust my senses
                         or beliefs—
                         or anyone again?

## Guilt

I think guilt must be the most difficult emotion for the survivors of suicide. It is so easy to blame ourselves, and it is so hard to let go of that last remnant of connection with the person we have lost, and so to finally say goodbye.

But it is guilt that will keep us from living, and if we give in to that, then we too have committed a kind of psychological suicide. And in a sense guilt puts a stain on the whole world.

When I was first told of Dick's note, indicating he would do harm to himself, my first words were words of guilt, "Oh, no—oh, God—I don't deserve to live. . . ." All I could think was that I had done it. Somehow I must have driven him to it, or not seen where he was headed.

113

For months I tried to feel his pain, tried to know how he must have felt. I tormented myself as much as I could and still remain functional. I felt my hair would turn gray and I would get cancer—and that it was what I deserved, though I never said that to anyone. It frightens me still to remember those thoughts, but helps me realize too how we do wish ourselves illness.

When I crossed the streets I hardly watched the cars. I just thought if they hit me I would be with Dick. The line between life and death seemed very thin to me then, and not frightening. I was surprised how close they seemed. It wasn't a chasm I feared to cross, but both seemed mixed together. Perhaps in a sense I was only half alive then, or maybe it is simply another state of awareness.

I went over everything in Dick's and my life together. At times we were close, other times not so close, but no matter what, I always felt it was part of the whole. I never doubted that. I felt we belonged together—that the ins and outs, the ebbs and tides were encompassed by love. I thought that circle could hold tears, angry words, and distance, as well as affection, laughter and joy. But now I built case after case against myself. Maybe I wasn't a good enough wife or friend? Had I been that lacking? Had I loved well enough? It must not have been enough, I would conclude. And yet all my questioning was self-centered. Basically I knew nothing I did or didn't do added up to what he did. One thing I knew. I didn't know him. I had no idea he was capable of even considering such an act. I had the fantasy we were so close, that we were truly bonded to one another. And I knew now there had been a gap.

I knew too, though, that his final act was one thing he couldn't have shared with me, because I would have fought to keep him alive, and he knew that. I would have clung to him, and not let him go. And he wanted to go. He wanted to die.

After a long while, I did wonder if he didn't have that right. This is easier for me to say in relation to myself, though, than it is when I think of Richard's loss, and still I know that Richard has new strengths now, and understanding and awarenesses because of it. I know that his destiny, too, is his own.

Journal excerpt, November 14, 1979:

. . . I know that if I could have stopped Dick I would have done almost anything within my power. But who would I be doing it for? Really myself. I am the one who didn't want to suffer the separation—the loss. So now I want to say to Dick—"I let you go."

I have more of a faith that there is an order in this universe of ours. It only looks like disorder, but time often cleanses our sight. Now the only judgment I can make is that it is very hard at the point of separation.

So I began to realize it was Dick's decision. No one else would have wanted that in any way. He did not tell a soul. He kept his secret, and made the choice, for reasons I can only speculate about now, and still the reasons don't really matter. People have said everything from "He was a saint and martyr" to "He was very sick." He did what he did, and in a way we have no right to interpret it. He did it for reasons he considered right and necessary—the only thing to do. In a way I feel—Can't he even have that?

If survivors get over the feelings of guilt, there are, I feel, always others who may still hold blame. It is again, I believe, something for those others to hang on to—to keep them, too, from the fear of the unknown, and to help them assimilate their loss, of a friend, or a member of mankind.

I know that the questions arose—Why couldn't she see what was happening? All I can say is that it is easy for others to ask that. We don't always know how to interpret behavior, and it is easy to look back and see what we might have done or seen. I saw questioning in some people's eyes after Dick's death, or sometimes I could feel it in their manner. Anger because of our own hurt and anguish cause us to want to place a "cause" somewhere.

Journal entry, June 29, 1979:

Have I been branded with guilt the rest of my life? Will I always bear the stigma of guilt by association? Will I be set free?

There is, I know, such a thing as justifiable guilt. If we have ever wished anyone harm on any level, felt angry or disgusted, or even unappreciative, then if that person commits suicide it confronts us as the furthest extension of our thoughts. Every time I was selfish, every time I wasn't as loving as I might have been, every time I took him for granted, these all came back to me. The more I believe our thoughts do affect others, the less release there is from blame.

On the other hand, I do feel we are too afraid of guilt. Maybe in some ways I was a co-creator in his death, though I didn't mean to be. Maybe I was also a co-creator of his happiness.

I think, in the final analysis, I have to listen to my heart and answer to it. I have to learn to forgive myself for not being all I could have been, to learn and grow and go on. We are all guilty and innocent, all victims, the one who died and the ones who must learn to live again.

Dick was always the one to talk me out of my guilt. Now I've had to work on it for myself. When we lost the baby in October, I started immediately to blame myself, to tell myself I shouldn't have been out shopping the day before the spotting started. Later I learned the baby not only was Down's syndrome, but also had another genetic defect that kept it from developing. Whether I ever find or know reasons for Dick's death I still have to accept all that has happened, be forgiving of myself and life and go on.

I do believe we are all responsible for our lives, and so acceptance of our involvement in what happens around us is essential, but I feel we have to also know and respect that others have their own ultimate choices, as we do ours. That is important too. It sounds like the old heredity versus environment argument. They are not mutually exclusive.

If we say we caused someone to do something, then we are playing God. On the other hand, we do affect one another, and regarding our own lives, perhaps we are God.

I think we need to realize the terrible power of our arguments and demands, and to realize the wonderful awesome power of our love, but I need to know I can never be everything to another, and one other person can never be everything to me. Each person has his or her own destiny.

116

That's the loneliness, but that's the hope and beauty too.

But I didn't know all of this before.

We always think we have forever, and we don't. I was so sure we would always be together, that he would always be there, that we would grow old together. There are so many things I wish I could have said to him, or shown him. For a long time I wished so much that, even if he couldn't be stopped from jumping, I could have talked to him for just an hour.

I think parts of me did symbolically die when Dick died, and parts of me eventually awakened. I couldn't see clearly many things I can see now. I couldn't see that I had everything. Sometimes I wanted love more than I wanted to give it, and I couldn't always fully appreciate the transitoriness of every-thing. I thought I was lacking when Johanna was born, and when she died. I thought I needed to possess love and people, and I held grudges and felt hurt by others often. Now I have let go of some of this. My needs are less. I feel I have a great deal. And I do.

So, can I forgive myself, and go on? If the old "I" died, then does this new "I" deserve to live—deserve to love again?

Dick used to say when he did good deeds for people, "Maybe they won't do the same back for me, but it's like I'm doing it in this big circle. They'll do something for someone else. It'll get back to me sooner or later."

Maybe all the good stuff didn't have time to get back to him, but I can try to pick it up from there.

Maybe I didn't see Dick's true needs. Maybe I could have loved better. But now I'll try to put clearer vision and love in that circle. And maybe I'll start with myself, and then let it go out from there, and hope it will travel to another and another. Maybe it'll come back to me, maybe it won't, and maybe I can learn to say, That's OK.

*Shame*

Shame, too, is something we often experience when some-one takes his or her life. People look away, avert their eyes—at least here in the Western hemisphere.

117

There is always an explanation due, or expected. Once the fact is known, then come the words "Why—what heppened?" If someone is hit by a car, or dies of physical illness, there may be an inner cry of "Why," they may question God, but no one questions the wife and children—or the parents.

Suicide so often connotes failure—a feeling of failure—and so the downcast eyes.

I don't feel Dick was a failure in any way. He couldn't or didn't want to cope with his world anymore. And who is to say he had no right, or even that it was a bad choice? Perhaps an unfortunate choice, but not a bad choice.

Shame is not a true emotion. It is only something we've learned. Since the Garden of Eden we've felt shame at our nakedness, at our exposure, at our vulnerability. Little children feel no shame until we teach it to them.

And so when someone is not perfect physically or emotionally in our eyes, we judge them "not whole"—or if they show us too much of themselves, we often look away, and want to cover up.

Shame must be the other face of pride, and I think the angels fell because of that.

It is just too bad that some things happen. It would have been a lot easier if they hadn't, but it's not ever shameful. With Johanna, instead of "How terrible—she's retarded," something in me wanted to say, "But see, a child is born."

And I want to say in regard to Dick—a man lived, and a man died, but life still is, and who he was in spirit still lives.

*Anger*

> Widow—widow—widow
> I want to bare my wound
> tear my chest
> let you see my gash.
> My husband's blood is on me.
> And on you.
> I want my pound of flesh.
>
> Widow—widow—widow
> A dark poisonous spider

118

is not me.
The king is dead
Long live the king,
but where is he?
Gone in a flash—
the man who fell to earth.

Your poem
too dramatic.
Why did you save it till the end?
The finale was too grand
Leaving only me to clap
to understand

It was your strongest work of art.
But didn't you know
one man's life is worth 10,000 poems?

(January 16, 1979)

Anger is a feeling I didn't and haven't felt consistently. It is hard to know who or what to be angry with, and yet it has woven its way through me. Anger can be very good at times. It can give some strength to get us through until a bit of real inner strength builds up. We can use it to protect ourselves, but it is important to be aware if we are doing that. Both guilt and anger are excesses of emotion our minds build cases around.

Anger is very evident in the poem I wrote. Anger often was more subtle, the kind of anger that didn't want me to look at pictures of Dick for several months. And sometimes anger was directed toward others.

It surfaced one day at work when I realized the folder I'd written in memory of Dick wasn't being circulated around my department—yet. I felt hurt that it could be considered so inconsequential. I interpreted that as—Dick was inconsequential, and maybe I was too. I felt anger, too, when I could see Richard's loneliness, and saw no one coming forward to give to him. I felt righteous anger when I realized the police had not thoroughly looked for Dick and had not taken even his notes seriously. They, in fact, I discovered later, had not "combed the campus," as they had told me they would.

"Three policemen," they said, "in between duties, looked for him. Other things took priority."

I had thought a man's life took priority.

"Most of the time," the police captain said, "things don't turn out this way."

So then I knew they had not taken his note seriously. How ironic—the campus where Dick always felt so many people didn't care enough about the things that mattered had acted as he would have expected. All I could think of was the button Dick always had pinned up on his desk. It said simply, "Give a damn."

I had anger every time I felt Richard and I were being treated in a less than kind way (this more in the early months), for I had no tolerance for hurt. It was enough. It was already too much. Anger played through me in a way that caused me to mistrust and to be very cautious.

And I had anger for the whole university system, and for all of us who couldn't see what was happening, and for the lack of space I felt was given a man . . .

But anger, even righteous anger, is fruitless. It has to be looked at, and resolved.

Some of the things that made me angry, I just had to deal with. For example, finding Richard a Big Brother healed that hurt I had for his loneliness. Some anger I had to just go past, or retreat from, as in the case of the police. It's over now. The lesson they must have learned is much greater than anything more I could say.

Some of the anger does come from the fear and the loss, and some of it is justifiable. The paradox is that death gives us anger, but that especially in the face of death, we should be able to go beyond it, and to reach some kind of peace in this, our limited time.

*Denial*

Is there such a thing? The word denial is a denial itself of belief and of hope. Who are we to say, for example, that when Richard spoke of Dick in the present tense for a while after

120

Dick's death, his view of reality was wrong? He knew Dick was not physically here, but perhaps he carried him inside. Who is to say which is more real?

I heard Richard Bach, author of *Illusions*, speak recently. He said if he were to see his best friend's plane flying along, and suddenly it exploded, his first reaction, and ours too, is always, "No, it didn't happen. I can't believe it!" And then, he says, we suppress that thought and convince ourselves, "Yes, it did happen." But Bach continued, "The first thought is our intuition—and that is right."

More and more, it seems we realize our vision is limited. We are taught to deny hope and love, but to be an artist in our lives is to perhaps trust our intuition, to not deny our inner self, or our inner vision.

Is Dick dead? Is there death? Of course in our reality this is so. He isn't here physically. He doesn't exist in this space or time.

I don't know any certain answers past that point.

I can live with the denial of finiteness, because I know that I don't know, but not with the denial of infiniteness. That door is open. I can even live with finality, if that is so, but I can't live with the denial of anyone's hope.

On another level, there has to be an acknowledgement of change, that things are never to be the same, and a riding with that.

C. S. Lewis expresses this idea of change in his small book, *A Grief Observed:*

Kind people have said to me "She is with God." In one sense that is most certain. She is, like God, incomprehensible and unimaginable.

But I find that this question, however important it may be in itself, is not after all very important in relation to grief. Suppose that the earthly lives she and I shared for a few years are in reality only the basis for, or prelude to, or earthly appearance of, two unimaginable, supercosmic eternal somethings. Those somethings could be pictured as spheres or globes. Where the plane of Nature cuts through them—that is an earthly life—they appear as two circles (circles are slices of spheres). Two circles that touched. But those two circles, above all the point at which they touched, are the very thing I am mourning for, homesick for, famished for. You tell me "she goes on." But my heart and body are crying out, come back, come back. Be a circle, touching my circle on the plane of Nature. But I know this is impossible. I know that the thing I want is exactly the thing I can never get. . . .

The denial of this change is what causes people to often avoid contact with those who have been touched by death. They feel uncomfortable with loss and with our earthly mortality.

A young widow I interviewed for a story once told me "I felt abandoned by most people, and it hurt a lot, until I realized I was a living example of what could happen to them."

When Johanna was only a few weeks old, I recall a woman admiring her, touching her little fingers and cooing at her. I felt obliged to tell the woman Johanna's difference. The woman drew back immediately, pulled attention and affection away, and said, "Oh, why did you tell me that?" I had blemished her reality. It was from then on that I did not tell anything to people who were not intimately involved. I wanted Johanna to have the love she drew from people. It was pure and had nothing to do with labels. I let it be.

But the withdrawal from the reality of physical death and from those we see as not perfect is a denial of life. They are withdrawing from a surface reality that we have to first accept, and then see beyond. Life as we know it does end. Some people do not fit into "normal" categories, but when we can't even accept that, we also close the door to mystery and beauty.

After the knowledge of change, the realization and the slow building of a different world begins. That's the transformation. That's the creative process. That's the acceptance, not only of loss, but of a new view and of new gains.

*The Searching/The Finding*

An attitude of wild hunting and searching came to me with Dick's death. The dreams every night—I would dream of putting my arms around him, telling him I loved him, but he would never respond. During the day I half expected his car to still drive up in front of the house, and while on the campus I kept expecting to see his familiar form striding toward me from a distance.

It is so unbelievable to realize someone has gone, that we'll never hear their voice, or touch their hand again.

I turned over every psychological leaf. I began to investigate every avenue, looking for answers. I guess I thought then I would have something. Detectives seek to solve the crime of murder. Suicide is perhaps the perfect murder. It can't ever really be solved, and maybe it isn't meant to be.

I went over every conversation we had. But none of them added up to what had happened. I talked to people at work who had known him, but all I saw in their faces was the same shock and hurt, puzzlement and guilt.

Talking to the campus police for the first time since that night was another facet of searching, as was returning to the place where it happened, and sending for the autopsy report, which I then realized I couldn't bear to read.

The subconscious hope, I suppose, is that somewhere along the line someone will say, it didn't really happen. I sometimes wonder if all this searching is really an innate belief in life. The knowledge of its cessation is incomprehensible. Even the atoms within particles of sand vibrate, they say. And so, when, if ever, does life cease?

Just recently, over one and one-half years later, I had another dream which shows me there is still a seeking part of me. I dreamed Dick and I were talking about all that happened since he left, how Richard had grown. Then I looked at him, and tried to fight back tears, and I said, "Don't ever do that again."

My outward seeking led me to talk to the woman from work with whom Dick had shared his painful thoughts of Johanna and his job situation. The seeking led me also to talk to a few other secretaries who had known Dick. All spoke highly of him. "He was the only personnel analyst worth anything," said one. "He cared, and he made stands, but no one backed him up."

But the search curves back on itself. Our thoughts are

curved, pointing to no answers, only more questions. And yet it's helped fill in my picture, part of the side of the man I didn't know.

That is the real sadness, I guess. We are all wholenesses that others never know, and we ourselves, cannot even grasp our own completeness. Maybe that's because we are never complete, always becoming.

As a good man I know once told me, "We are all trying to find our way home," and I guess that is it. We think if we are truly close to another person we touch home, or if we marry, or have a child. Some people try to touch home with drinking or drugs. Sometimes we seek it in music, art, or looking at a sunset. And the truth is we do catch glimpses of it, but I don't know if anyone really gets there. I know I haven't. I think life is that seeking.

Now, Dick's search is over. Dick went home. Too early, we could say. Perhaps, but only he knew that. Now the search is mine, not the search for his answers anymore, but the search for mine, and the path to my own way home.

# 12 / The Early Months—Beginning

The cord was cut. Now there was no fighting the onset of transition. My house reflected that I must be in transition, or in a cocoon state. It was more cluttered than it had ever been. I'd never liked it that way, but somehow it felt more comforting to me than order would have. I tried to keep things somewhat neat, but psychologically I seemed to need everything around the way a pack rat does.

I needed to build a nest. Clutter at that point was comforting.

One day I decided I should put out some of Dick's clothes for Goodwill. I didn't at that point want to give much of anything away—only T-shirts, underwear, and socks; and I had put in the house shoes he had worn much of the time. I drove off to work that day, after setting the bags on the front step. Then about a mile from home terrible guilt feelings overtook me. How could I give them away? I didn't want those shoes, but somehow they symbolized Dick, I guess. I drove back and took them out of the sack. I just couldn't do that yet.

This early time was a time of hanging on, in more ways than

125

one—to Dick, to pain, to others, and to myself, but little by little I also found what could help start to make a pathway.

The most important thing to me was the contact with people. It was necessary and vital. Warm human voices and personalities, just being near, or present, touching my hand, hugging me—desperately were needed, but not always available.

During this time, Ed, Dick's coworker, came one day with a box holding Dick's belongings from work. It is so strange to see a box full of a person's little world, the world that reflected that person, now lifeless, now a box of clutter: photos, watercolors, a little wood sculpture Richard had made in an art class, a ceramic sea otter, the button saying, "Give a Damn," a little vase a secretary had given him, and a book—a book I'd never heard him mention reading. It was Alexander Solzhenitsyn's *One Day in the Life of Ivan Denisovich*. And there was an envelope containing a note I had written Dick one day, after we had lunch on campus near the eucalyptus trees. I had pasted a leaf on the note, and mailed it to him at his office. I had done it in almost a teasing way, and still it had meant enough to him that he had kept it. I put the box in the garage. It seemed somehow wrong to touch these belongings—so personal—this select collection of a life.

In a month, an architect friend suggested to me that he wanted to put together an invitational stained glass show in memory of Dick. When the day came for the show I could hardly believe how beautiful it was. Dick's pieces were placed in a specially constructed area in the lobby: his oval shape, ". . . and a space"; an art nouveau floral design; a seagull; an art-deco sunset constructed in the frame of an old window; and an exquisite butterfly he had made for me, which now when I looked at it looked like a man with wings. In other rooms of the office suite brilliant works of stained glass by other artists were hung. The afternoon sun filtered through them. Colors and light cascaded over the one hundred or more friends who attended. I felt I was inside a giant many-faceted jewel. The feelings were high and not sad. The beauty took it above all of that, but as the afternoon ended, a grayness covered me as everyone left. People went off together, in groups of two, three, four. Pieces of cheese, empty plastic wine glasses still sat here and there. My friend and his partner started cleaning up. I sat for a few minutes. Now I still had to go home, and now, still, no one was at home. An aching filled my throat. No one really knew. The word "widow" means "empty" in Sanskrit, and that is exactly the way I felt for a long time. Aside from the pain of why Dick did it, and the pain of trying to identify with his suffering, was just the pain of being alone.

The phone rang in the house several times a day for the first few weeks. I would talk until my voice ached. I needed that talking, that telling and retelling of the events. When I told the story to others, I was telling the story to myself. Though the story was no longer the event, though there were no answers to my questions, at least it was something. I could hang on to the story, say his name—and so in a sense I still had Dick, and I was making the event real. After a few weeks, calls stopped, but needs to be in touch remained.

The most appreciated gift friends could give me was just to be there. Some disappointed me. Others that I wouldn't have expected to came forward. People who *could* be with me *were* with me. There is a rightness in that. At times there were phone conversations where ten-minute spaces elapsed. Words can only say so much. We were together, connected in silence by a telephone, by caring.

It seems such a simple thing, such a mundane thing, but I cherish friends who took Richard and me to dinner, or invited us to their homes for dinner. Food and friendship are full of life. A special emptiness, particularly at the ritual of dinner-time, reigns in a house emptied by someone's dying. Life felt cold, little nourished. It helped to be out of the house and in warm, caring, life-supporting surroundings, because we lived on the edge of darkness.

Journal entry, January 23, 1979:
I feel emotional, hurt, drained, all day. I feel hurt and yet I can't believe I deserve to take care of myself, to heal. It's hard to nurture myself.

It was winter, and though in southern California it isn't often extremely cool, this winter seemed more intense, and it suited me just fine. It rained a lot—everything was gloomy and overcast for days at a time. It seemed to go on forever, and it felt right to me.

But I tried to stay above the storm. I didn't want to be lost in it. It was a time to be distracted by busyness or fantasy—movies, plays—or to be soothed by music or a glass of wine. I welcomed anything to blot out the pain for a little while in those first few months. Escape can be misused, but there is a place for it too. There would be other times, later, for introspection, for sorting out guilt and loss.

My job was a blessing. It was essential to have to get out of bed every day and have someplace I needed to be. The importance or unimportance of tasks I dressed for didn't matter. My friends at work filled in my life every day. They provided the nest, without which I don't know how I could have gone on.

Somehow during this time I managed to write an article on widowhood for a local newspaper. I recall that beginning this article was so important to me. My real work, writing, has always given me strength. Someone said to me—you won't finish that—widows start a lot of things and don't finish them. But I knew I would. It was essential to me.

In January, two months after Dick's death, I began teaching a class in creative writing through Community College for the first time. I was terrified that first night the class came in. I just didn't think I could handle this now, though I had wanted it before, last year, when I had applied. I knew, though, if I didn't take on the class I might lose my chance. It turned out to be, and still is, one of the best things I've ever done. Each week I had to direct my energies outward, past myself. I had to find new ideas, organize my thoughts, and give to those people in the class—listen to them, try to see how to guide, help, and inspire them. It was like magic, because what happened is they indirectly guided, helped, and inspired me. No one knew what had happened to me. They accepted me in the role of "teacher" at face value, and I was only myself there, with none of the shadow of what had happened. I found myself genuinely interested in trying to draw them out, and genuinely thrilled when they wrote something that communicated.

It was important, too, to get my body going—to exercise, and move. I went to a gym for a while, and then to a dance class. I had almost forgotten to move. It also helped bring about a better frame of mind. Feeling tired and getting into a Jacuzzi at the gym relaxed and soothed me, and so also helped.

For months it was just a simple time, a slow-building, basic time—like the bottom rung of Abraham Maslow's pyramid. My infant soul sought only security, comfort, release from pain. It was a bare beginning time. A time to hold back the horror, to hold on, and just keep going, trusting time to lead me.

During those early days, letters from friends and acquaintances were wonderful messages. I felt held up and supported by the sea of letters. Messages from people I hadn't heard from for years helped make real that it all had existed, and that it all had ended. Even as surely as everything changes, love and caring can fill in a space and erase distance and time. The letters were like leaves falling from the tree that had been our life. They expressed feelings for Dick:

Dick was often sensitive and understanding to me, and often helped me to feel better. At times I could help him too, but did not always recognize the need, and there was no sure way to see the need. . . . I will remember the good times. . . .

I wish I could have stood with the other "Gallery" members Sunday as a show of the lasting friendships that were established during those years. . . .

My memorial to Dick maybe could be more poetically expressed by my playing the "Moonlight Sonata" than by my fumbling with words here. But I celebrate his soul, even though it was clouded the last few months by deep sorrow. He had a refreshing sense of humor, a zest for adventure in living, a sensitivity to people, a willingness to help, a set of values that was based on the search for truth in ideas and hearts, not in material possessions.

I came to respect him for his sensitivity to beauty, his intelligence and his integrity. What can I say but to acknowledge I was unable to realize the pain he was in. . . .

We loved that guy. We have only the fondest memories of him as always being a sweet and happy person. . . . Dick was a friend, the kindest of men, and we miss him.

The letters hurt and helped at the same time.

I tried to think of activities to keep Richard as happy as possible. Part of this meant being together. In the early months we both needed time to lean on each other, to know we would both be there for each other.

Richard said one day, after driving home from a get-together with friends, "It's good we can go out. At least we are functioning." Pretty perceptive for a twelve year old.

Along with the comfort and pleasure I felt being invited to be with people, was the exclusion and extreme sensitivity I felt when we weren't included.

Hearing people talk of plans to be together, all I could think was, can't you see how much we need to be with people? Can't you see we are cut off and alone? I felt like a child thrown out in the snow, grateful even for matches to light small fires. I could see life was still all around me, but I felt we didn't live in it, and only at times were invited to participate in it.

Though it would have been hard, it would have been good for me to ask for time with people. Sometimes others don't know what we need, and yet I found it difficult to reach out because I had such a feeling of wounded vulnerability, even to those people who sent notes, telling me to call them.

Journal entry, December 16, 1978:
How are things today? Just baby steps. Walking, not running. Sometimes smiling for a second or two. Not laughing—wondering if joy will ever come again, if only

for a visit. Keeping the door closed, can't let anything in, or it may all come in on me. My rational mind wonders if anyone can ever bear this. It is so horrible—so *still* shocking and unbelievable.

Along with the feeling of separation, there was a slight feeling of paranoia. Though I had never been especially fearful before, now I was afraid every night. I'd sleep with the hall light on, would check all the doors to see if they were bolted. Almost as if it were a self-fulfilling prophecy I received two obscene phone calls, and then one day came home from work to find our house had been broken into—for the first time—and this after I had installed a dead bolt and peep hole. Someone had gone through all the drawers in the bedroom and in my desk.

I had in general a feeling of mistrust, of unsafeness. In time these feelings passed. They are alien to the person I basically am, but it is amazing how easy it is to slip into that state of mind. The truth is we can't really protect ourselves anyway, and so there is nothing to do but trust.

Any kind of death or separation is a shock to our systems. The best thing I could do, anyone can do, is to be kind to ourselves, and most of all to try to participate in life as much as possible.

Being able to express myself was also one of the best helps for me. I am lucky I can talk, paint, and write about feelings.

Writing is my best tool. It saved me with Johanna, and it is saving me now. It helps me to somehow rise above the confusion. They say we are in a different brain pattern when we write—theta. Our deeper subconscious helps us to assimilate and transform, to create and go beyond. Expression, creativity, transformation. Disorder and turmoil turn into at least the illusion of order. This helped me transform what seemed outwardly horrible into something bearable. All my life that has been my one constant—ever since my father used to bring me reams of paper home from his office. As a child I drew and wrote poems on that paper. That expression has been more steady than children, husband, mother, father, or even God, and still sometimes I think maybe that expression is God.

131

Journal entry, February 4, 1979:
The writing, coming, will free me—I need help coming to terms with tragedy—my tragedy—Dick's tragedy—why, why—why not?—He let go of life—of me—his life—our child—What could ever be that bad? I thought we had a good life—thought he was just in a bad mood—could I have helped if he'd given me the chance?

I made the brochure and card in memory of Dick, which I sent to friends. I kept a journal, and though poems didn't come as often as they used to—and I almost thought for a while they might never come again—in time they began to fall from me every now and then.

There is another subtle facet of art which I truly believe, and it is that we can do many things symbolically in art and poetry—acts and thoughts we don't have to actually materialize in "real" life. A person can commit suicide symbolically in a poem or a painting, and then maybe it doesn't have to be done in actuality.

The expression of an experience helps each of us to be more aware of that experience, and that is what helps us assimilate it. Things, I believe, have to be dredged up, looked at, made conscious, and then somehow transformed or assimilated.

I believe art not only helps us dredge up material, but the form we shape it into can also help us.

During this early time I also found myself going to a woman who was a "psychic" counselor, for the first time. I had gone to Los Angeles to meet with my good friend Christy. Christy had been to visit the woman before. Though this was a realm I had never really explored or known much about, I felt very open and accepting of the fact that there is much more than I know.

The woman asked for something of Dick's to hold in her hand. I gave her his wedding ring. She closed her eyes for a minute, and then she said, "Dick's suicide was the first thing he ever did totally for himself. It was his privilege to go where he has gone." Her voice was gravelly and strange, and I wasn't sure what to think, but her insights seemed to fit. She told me I had completed an entire lifetime that included Dick and

132

Johanna and Richard—that this time was completely over, and now a new life was beginning, and it was for me and it included Richard.

Before we left, she said, with a smile on her face, "The way he did it was very beautiful, you know. He flew. He was a bird. He felt freedom." I looked at her cautiously. I wanted to believe this.

This experience helped me find a beginning of release. It, too, was part of going on. Though I knew there were no answers, maybe now I was looking for purpose, or order. The hunting and searching—a lot of the turmoil—was beginning to be over.

I tried to begin to set the stage to heal, to let go of the past and the hurt, and to realize I wasn't in the cold, to begin to make sense of my world. I know deep inside we are all connected to life as surely as life is a part of all of us. There aren't really any separations, but loss causes us to believe there are.

The early days were like a bridge I was building, spanning the life I'd lost and the new life still ahead somewhere. The early days were days of limbo. These were the days of survival.

> Eight months now
> you've been gone.
>
> New light falls
> on the floor,
>
> luminous shafts form streaks
> across linoleum and rug.
>
> This light doesn't expect you,
> doesn't know you.

(July 23, 1979)

133

# 13 / Therapists

Hoping and waiting for contact with friends, spending some time at work and with writing wasn't enough, though. Especially when I thought of Richard. I knew I just wasn't certain about the progress of his grief. I decided it could be helpful to find a therapist for him to talk to a few times.

I knew I didn't have the words, or the courage, to really talk about what had happened with Richard yet. I couldn't really help him in his pain. My own was too great.

Finding help for Richard also gave to me. An objective, knowledgeable person could, I felt, help with insights to support us in dealing with such a loss. I felt some hope in seeking this. At least I had the fantasy someone was there.

This, too, formed part of the bridge.

I took Richard to the Child Guidance Clinic of a nearby hospital. He sat in the small office while the doctor questioned him and tried to show friendliness. Richard just looked down. Afterwards he said he didn't want to come anymore—that he didn't like the man. Feeling it might just be his reluctance to talk about himself or his feelings, I said, "Are you sure,

Richard?" But after three visits (almost dragging him to the last one) I didn't take him there anymore. I felt concerned about what the loss and shock, especially the way it had happened, could do to him, but this endeavor didn't seem to be getting us anywhere.

One day I talked with a psychologist at UCSD. He said he knew a doctor who was wonderful with children, that this man headed a clinic during the week, but saw a few patients on the weekends at his home—a ranch with horses and dogs.

This doctor, he said, walks around outside with those children who come to him, and they talk. It is such a simple departure from the usual environment of patient/doctor, but it seemed it might make a world of difference.

He agreed to see Richard, and so one Saturday morning we drove to his home, through the green countryside. Richard took to him immediately. I could see in Richard's eyes the halting acceptance and the glimmer of good rapport. In the weeks that followed he looked forward to these visits, and so did I, because it felt like hope and another step on.

A few minutes were always spent with me just before we left, and the doctor explained to me what they had talked about and what happened.

Much of the time, aside from occasionally walking outside, a variety of games were played. The games were a tool to establish relationship. They provided a non-threatening backdrop to casual, revealing talk. Sometimes the two would wrestle and the doctor would say to Richard, "Pretty soon you'll be able to beat me, or some other man, the same way you would have beat your dad." And so they played out some of the behavior patterns Richard would have played out with Dick.

The doctor told me that though Richard did not talk a lot about what happened, he was able to discuss it. Establishing this good, warm relationship with a man Richard trusted was probably as important as how much they discussed the difficult situation. Yet there was openness to it, so when it bubbled up, they could talk.

I know it gave Richard a good feeling to have someone take interest in him, and to have someone to talk to when he didn't or couldn't talk to me.

135

After a few months of these talks, either once a week or twice a month, we stopped going. Richard was calmer, and he was enthusiastic and involved in sports and in school. There weren't any signs that indicated any specific problems. I was told Richard had assimilated it remarkably well, under the circumstances, and that something like this is handled by a child or young person in a much different way than an adult might suspect.

"Children often just put it off to the side, as if in a separate box. It's not as if they suppress it. They know it is there. They just don't know quite what to make of it, or how to handle it. They are not emotionally mature enough to go through the same sort of grieving process adults do." He then said to call or come back anytime we needed to talk more. I felt a sense of security having a resource like this man.

We did make an extra trip back out one day. The horse they had often walked out to see had just given birth to a beautiful little colt. Richard fed the mother some hay, and we watched as the small colt, with its fragile strength and warm soft eyes, sought nourishment from her.

The doctor told us as we left that establishing a good relationship with a therapist is one of the main things he hoped to accomplish with Richard.

"This sort of relationship," he said, "can often be a help."

I realized Dick had never experienced that—never put that kind of trust in anyone. Is that why he turned to no one? Deep inside he must have felt no one could help, or perhaps he didn't want help. I wonder too—when our mothers answer and comfort us when we are small, does that give us faith there is help, that someone is there? I always survive, and I always believe help is available. I know the answers are always inside, but if I'm desperate, I'll seek someone to talk to, and Dick never did.

I did feel desperate soon after Dick's death, and I also felt I needed a place to cry, and so I also went to a psychiatrist for a few weeks. Each time I just came in, sat down, cried, and said all the lost crazy things I had to say. Mostly he just listened. I felt I was basically talking to myself, and I think it is what I needed at the time. After Christmas I didn't go back because I guess I felt that part of the storm was over.

136

Later though, during the following summer, I once again went to a counselor. This man felt more like a "professional friend," and his slightly Eastern approach seemed right for me. I still felt a desire to talk about Dick, but this time I wanted to talk more about our marriage. It was as if I had to finish the relationship alone. And so I went to finish some more, and I think that is just the way it is—we just keep finishing, and it takes a long time for it really to end. With this man I could put everything more in perspective. I began to learn the beginning of acceptance, of just letting it be. He helped me to live in the present more, helped me realize I have my own destiny, and that Dick did too.

Journal entry, September, 1979:
Therapist says I must realize Dick only exists in my thoughts. I must know *now* is all. I believe that, but I also believe everything we've known still exists. Time isn't linear—it's a circle—but I suppose it is a matter of how much we can handle.

I feel we find in others a portion of what we are seeking. They can help fill in a puzzle piece here and there. Eventually we come to those persons who light the road for us. Many people would not seek this kind of help. I sought it as a source of security and clarity. The fact that we are so emotion-trained, that we can cry in front of the proper professional person, and often not in front of a friend, is due not so much to the way we compartmentalize our lives, as it is to the way a therapist can see the anguish and still stay objective. We can depend on him or her to see us through. There is something more positive and mutual which seems appropriate to share with friends. I didn't feel my pain was something I wanted to give a friend, even if I could have. In a sense too I did turn to therapists because I felt at that point there was really no one else to turn to, in that way, and it was important at a certain stage of loneliness to turn to someone, to learn to cope. I think it is important to come in contact with whatever and whomever can guide us on—our friends, teachers, doctors, our children, and ourselves through our inner listening, creativity and expression.

Though writing has always been my best therapy in the long

137

run, this was a time when I guess I desperately needed outside nurturing, and so I stumbled around, grasped, and tried to find a little of it.

The therapist–patient relationship is limited though. It is for the embryo stage of a soul, yet every stage is important—every step, every key, every light switch. Therapy is not to teach us how to fly, but to teach us how to walk.

I remember the words of a folksong I heard in the late 60's. The words, in effect, were:

> If you can't fly—run!
> If you can't run—walk!
> If you can't walk—crawl!
> Any old way you can make it baby,
> Keep on moving it along.

# 14 / Family and Friends

Everything had been blown apart. All relationships were changed. Some people came into focus, others faded, and my whole concept of family and friends was transformed. My friends became my family, and my family became my friends. Is blood thicker than water? Is anything thicker than love?

We had always been a small family, just the three of us. Now with only Richard and me left, we were not only a very small group, but a very off-balance one. There was a feeling of lack, along with the sorrow. Contact with other family members, with relatives, didn't fill the gap.

Contact with relatives was minimal. Dick's parents went to Mexico immediately after his death. They had planned the trip for months, and they thought, too, the change would be good. I'm sure they needed time to begin to assimilate their own incredible shock and pain, and I think, too, it would have been too hurtful to all be together. As with Johanna, this pain did not draw people together, but shook us all to our roots, and the need was to build from the inside out.

139

My own parents were no longer alive. I found myself missing the feeling of "mother," though I had seldom thought of my mother much for years. It's funny the way shock can throw a person back. My only relative was my brother, and strangely enough even that relationship fell apart for a time. We all had too much emotion, so that a small disagreement was blown out of proportion. So, at a time when I felt a lack, there was even more of a space. Eventually I could see it as a space to grow in, but not for a while.

We did spend that first Christmas with Dick's brother's family in Illinois for a few days, and that helped get us through that holiday. Planning for the trip, only six weeks after Dick's death, was what I needed—a reason to make lists, and then progress through those lists, a kind of mechanical way of living, but the best I could do at the time. I bought presents for Tom, his wife, Pat, for their children, bought snow gloves for Richard, wool socks, and on and on. My friends at work helped me get ready. I borrowed snowboots from one, a coat from another.

It was something to do. It was an aim. There was no real involvement or interest, but feeling aimless was frightening. There was too much fear and shock to handle much more than rote thinking. It was hard to know what to do every day. Getting through the day was the main thing.

In Illinois, Tom met us at the airport and drove us to their home past bleak snow-covered terrain. Leafless black trees lined the horizon as if they had been sketched in. Pat and Tom's home is an old farmhouse—small, cabinlike, rustic. It was warm and cozy inside, but the coldness in my heart could only respond minimally. In a way it felt like a dream, or a TV show, no more real than "Little House on the Prairie."

Journal entry, December 23, 1978:
We are at Pat and Tom's. Night before last I dreamed Dick and I lived in a very large house—so big—one room perfect for a baby. I went to Dick. It seemed we could have made love. . . . Then he pushed me away—said he didn't want anything to do with me. Then I looked in another room. There was another woman. I knew she was

140

waiting for Dick. I think this woman was Death. . . . We needed something—a move, a new house, a baby, a trip—not a suicide.

The days passed. Pat invited friends over to decorate the tree. Richard went snowmobiling. We visited Field Museum, went shopping and to restaurants. The talk wove in and out—about everyday matters, or about Dick. One day other relatives came from Mishawaka—Dick's grandmother and his favorite uncle. The talk was only surface—it was like a buzzing of bees, going around and around, afraid to settle. I said to John, Dick's uncle, "If you want to know anything, you can ask me." Then I showed him the folder I had made in Dick's memory. It told briefly what happened. In it I spoke of the things Dick loved, and a little about what he was like. It broke the ice. The buzzing settled. John nodded. He read the words, and said they helped. Then he spoke a little of earlier times when he had known his nephew. His eyes filled with sadness.

I knew it was harder for others to bring up the subject—of Dick, of death, and most of all, of suicide. I was the main source for that information. I had suffered the harshest shock, along with Richard. There was no way at this point to hurt us anymore. I had to be the one to open the door. In those early days, I could do it easier than I could later when the wound began to close. With time I became more reluctant to dig into it again.

All these people were kind to Richard and to me, and made us feel welcome, but inside I wondered, What does family really mean? Dick had been our family. Aloneness was all I could feel. Though I was with Dick's family, they were just that—his family. I had been around them very little, really. The fact they were relatives had no real meaning for me ultimately. Dick, Richard, and I had accepted each other, loved without reason, unconditionally. We belonged together. There was not this feeling of "otherness" which I felt now, though it was no one's fault.

Christmas Eve everyone was in the living room—Pat, Tom, their children, their neighbors. The Christmas tree glowed; presents and crumpled paper covered the floor; eggnog, food,

141

and laughter filled each person. But I felt separate, as if enclosed in a glass bubble. I sought contact with something else—a memory, a stillness. All the joy there was making me lonely. I went into the den and sat by the fire. I wanted to be there. I wanted to be with myself. I wanted to think about Dick. He was still too much a part of me. It had only been six weeks, and it was the first Christmas in nineteen years we hadn't been together. I looked into the fire, and then I started to cry. And it felt good. I wanted to cry. And I wanted to be where I was—by myself for a few minutes. Then Pat walked by, noticed me, came over, put her arms around me, and said, "Hey, none of that." It was a caring gesture, and it is hard to know what anyone really wants or needs, and yet it is OK to let someone cry and know tears are not bad. They can be cleansing and renewing.

Journal entry, Christmas Day, 1978:
Last night had another denial dream. I thought in my dream that if I wrote Dick a long letter and told him I loved him, he would come back—and I wanted that so much.

I cried last night—Christmas Eve—I felt he did care for all my past hurts—that he wanted to be the person who healed them. Then when I seemed to not need that, he felt a failure. . . . Did he feel he was denying me if he wasn't a "success"?— But he denied me by dying.

To Richard the Kenyon family are part of his blood, and I think their existence gives him some sense of belonging, though miles separate us. Tom was his dad's brother. "Tom looks just like Dad," Richard has said. There is a resemblance, but they were totally different people, with different values and ideas about how to live their lives. The very fantasy Richard carried about Tom, especially during that visit, did give him comfort, but hurt him, too, because to Tom, Richard is his nephew, and in no way is this comparable to being his son. He cares for Richard, but what does that mean in terms of actual contact? Caring, even long-distance, is important, but a

142

boy without a father indulges in many unfulfilled yearnings that may never be met.

When we left Chicago, and the plane lifted off the ground, Richard felt the separation from Tom, and most of all from Dick. The dreams wouldn't come true. His mouth turned down at the corners, and tears began to roll down his cheeks. "I miss somebody," he said, "and I don't even know who."

"Don't you think it's Dad?" I said.

And he nodded.

I put my arms around him and held him all the way to Tucson. He was twelve years old, no longer a little boy, but a long way from being a man. He was going to have to learn about being a man from assorted role models now, and there wouldn't ever be one man who cared for him and idolized him the way no one, but a father, can his only son, though I hoped there would be other men, who, in new ways, would care for him.

I know in my heart that quality is more important than quantity. Richard had a wonderful father for twelve years, who loved him very much, but to this day it is still hard for me to say that to Richard, because it still is painful.

Once back in San Diego, I was glad to go back to my job. My coworkers and the graduate students in the philosophy department where I worked were my family at that time.

They didn't judge or find fault. They accepted, cared in their way, treated me tenderly as if I had been seriously wounded. They gave me strength and a feeling of belonging that I could then bring home to Richard.

My own brother, Bud, and his wife, Marcia, were very present in the beginning, coming in the middle of the night when Dick didn't come home. Immediately after Dick's death my brother wanted to protect us and himself too from hurt, for he, too, was hurt by Dick's death, I know. Bud urged me within a few days to take Dick's belongings from the bedroom, to at least clear off the top of the dresser. I tried to do a little of this, but it was not easy to put away life as I knew it, and all that was left of Dick. My brother was anxious for me to get through it because he cared, but the other truth is that I'm sure he feared feeling responsible for us, and I think now maybe this is a major flaw in family relations. It can cause people to feel obligation. Since Bud was now the closest male, it seemed logical to him that he should bear some of the burden. Since he didn't especially want to do this, on top of his own family responsibilities, it probably felt to him that it was essential for me to hurry through this grief. The truth is, we were all in shock. The other truth is that he didn't need to be any more responsible than anyone else.

A few weeks later Marcia came to spend the weekend, with her son, Joel, twelve, and Caitlin, their then two year old, and Betsy, only a few months old (born exactly one month after Dick's death). We had never quarreled before, but we did that weekend, and I think the surface reasons for it are not even the issue. The insanity and emotions of the whole situation caused everything to go off balance. It caused a deep rift between me and my brother's family that lasted approximately ten months. As I think back, I realize now that at the time it happened I was too wounded to tolerate any distress. I needed to be around people who were kind to Richard and to me, who accepted us, and who could even nurture us. But that is asking a lot. Everyone can't give that. Eventually I learned to try to be with people who could give that until I was stronger and could stand on my own.

That night I felt everything had been finally taken from me—the floor had crumbled beneath. I felt tormented and punished by life. I became hysterical for the first and, I hope, last time in my life. I felt I couldn't survive, except by sheer will. I ran next door to my neighbors', to Joe and Monika's. They always were there for me, though we had never been close before Dick's death. It was and still is unbelievable to me that they opened their lives to Richard and me so totally after Dick's death, but that is exactly what they did. It seems to me now that perhaps this sort of good will is always waiting under the surface, and sometimes it just takes great pain to allow us to break through and give to each other. They let me in that night, asking no questions. I sat down on the couch, still crying, and Monika put the kettle on for tea. I felt horribly, physically ill. My head screamed, I felt dizzy and sick. I felt I wanted to die. I had reached the bottom. I felt a final severing. I knew for

144

certain now it was just Richard and me alone. I knew no one put us first—no one would take care of us. I had to take care of us both, like the song, "you and me against the world." And I think I truly became committed to the thought that night. It may have been a selfish resolution, but it was the first step of a new life. It was necessary at that point. When I reached that bottom, I became resolved to somehow make it. I had to finally realize there was no one, before I could later see that, in a way, there is everyone, that there are some very special friends, and that it is maybe "you and me with the world." I know now we can't expect certain things of people. They can't always give us what we need or want, but that doesn't mean we aren't given to, and that doesn't mean that we, too, can't give.

I had felt the world would be a little extra kind to us because we had suffered, and in some ways it was, but the most important thing is that we had to be extra kind to ourselves, to try to be patient, and to heal ourselves. It wasn't that so little was given, but that so much was needed. So I avoided situations or people I found too painful. I began to guard myself. I had to. I had no extra resource to deal with difficult situations inside, and I had no rock of stability, no confidence, no feeling of wholeness inside myself, or outside myself, to lean on, or depend on then.

Months passed.

The bridging of the chasm then existing between my brother and his family and Richard and me depended so much on my being able to let go of the hurt I was so tenaciously hanging onto. For some reason I couldn't, though I knew in my heart I wanted to. Finally in October of '79, almost a year after Dick's suicide, I heard a doctor named Paul Brenner talk. He has gone beyond traditional medicine, is a believer in alternative and holistic approaches, and he believes in love as the greatest healer. I had really gone to hear Elisabeth Kubler-Ross, but Paul was also on the schedule. I think I was meant to come that day to hear him because what he said went straight to my heart. The words shot through me. I decided to drop him a note, to tell him how he affected me.

This I did, not expecting an answer. He invited me to come

145

talk with him, and as we sat in his backyard on a beautiful sunny day, I related, among other things, the hurt and anger I felt being so estranged from Bud and his family. Paul said, "You'd feel terrible if something happened to your brother." And he said, too, "Just send love to your brother, whether it comes back or not."

Other people had told me, "You need to make contact with your brother," but I held onto the anger, didn't want to be the first one to reach out. I guess I wanted an apology, an eye for an eye.

But when I talked to Paul, and he said the words to me, I saw then for the first time that none of that mattered. A wall fell down, and I could see clearly, and it wasn't such a big wall after all. A little puff, a few words, and it was gone. But I had held onto it, and gritted my teeth, with all my might until that day.

I came home, wrote my brother—not an angry letter, not a letter going into the past at all, just an ordinary letter about what we were doing.

Journal entry, October 4, 1979:
Paul, by talking to me, has changed my heart about Bud. I could let go of the pain, and send love.

A month later my brother called me. He said, "Karen, I don't know why I haven't called. I think about you almost every day."

And I said, "I understand. I haven't had the courage to call you either."

And so the bridge was there again. It was OK.

In fact it was wonderful to be in touch again. Now we've all spent time together. We've not gone over the past. We've just gone on from where we are. Caitlin was then three, but she still remembered Richard, and Betsy had changed a lot, from three months to being a one year old.

I guess when emotions have been pushed to extremes, we often react in chaotic ways—everything clashes, is in turmoil, and out of tune. I've been told since then that it is very common during grieving periods for families to break apart, especially when the death is as sudden and emotion-charged as

146

a suicide. It seems so ironic to think that just when we need each other the most we are at odds. But the truth I guess is that we don't need each other so much as we need ourselves. When I could come to terms inside, and was back in tune and more whole within myself, I could be in touch with others.

I needed to learn to survive emotionally on my own, with Richard. So I believe it was a gift to me that the break-up with my brother occurred. It cut another cord. It gave me a space to live in and grow in. It gave me a chance to know and depend on myself. And now it is a gift to me that the gap is healed.

During the split Richard always seemed to have trust that it would all be OK someday. He missed Caitlin, because she was always very special to him, but he never seemed to have any angry feelings once he could no longer see her. He just wished it would be all right again, so that we could all be together.

Certain friends, at different levels of closeness, were almost a family to us during that first year. Though no one was really up close, there were people in close proximity. One friend took me to a writers' group to encourage my craft, another took Richard to a few ball games.

Larry offered to discuss financial decisions or any other decisions with me. Mary brought her sleeping bag for the first weekend I had to spend alone and just slept on the couch. We built a fire that night and watched a Chuck Mangione concert on TV. I cried and all I could think was—"Why did you go, Dick? You would have liked this! Didn't you know that?" Other friends occasionally invited Richard and me to their homes those first few weeks—and there were others: Val, who burglar-proofed our house after the burglary; Stefanie, who shared some of her writings and thoughts and special friends with me; and my friends in the philosophy department where I worked—Gale, Catherine, and June, who listened to me every day at work when I needed a compassionate ear; and Herbert Marcuse, the well-known philosopher-professor, who gave me inspiration and insight. I truly don't believe I could have survived without these friends from work. Without them I don't think I could have made it. They, along with Joe and Monika, my neighbors, came most intimately into our lives during those early broken months. These people were simply

147

there for us. To them I will forever be grateful, and forever feel they are *friend*. It is interesting, too, that except for a couple of wonderful exceptions, it was not the old friends, but it was new friends who became a part of us and a part of our new life.

It was just a new world. Everyone had to adjust. Everything had died really, not just Dick, but Richard's and my whole way of life.

So now I think "family matters" only in the sense that some people do matter, and some of those people may happen to be in our family.

Now I feel more love for family *and* friends. With less expectation there is more acceptance. We all interacted in this drama in the only way we knew how, and it's changed us all.

It is amazing how much of a change the loss of one person can bring about, how much of a space one person can leave.

Richard had a lot of needs. Little bits of male companionship helped, and a mosaic of broken pieces can glitter in a sort of wholeness of its own, but I wished he had more. I wished that after feeling loss and sadness he could have some joy and fulfillment. Miraculously that wish did come true. After someone mentioned Big Brothers of America to me I contacted the organization. Though several hundred boys are waiting here in San Diego, we were very lucky. Whatever luck is, whatever chance is, sometimes it seems to work for us. Within a few weeks Richard was matched with a Big Brother. Steve Reizner, Richard's Big Brother, is a truly special person. He spends time each week with Richard. Richard and I both have changed because of his entrance into Richard's life. He came in closely, a step closer than friendship. The two developed a real relationship, a knowing of each other—a being together. Richard has become more peaceful, less anxious, more sure of himself. For me, it seemed to set things more in place, and I like, too, the gentle, caring intelligence of this man, qualities not unlike Dick's. I like his influence on Richard. To Richard he is a great pal, someone to whom he is special, someone who won't suddenly go away, and that is what is so extraordinary.

This, too, has to do with family, or with brotherhood in the true sense.

The thing Richard seemed to miss the most for a long time was the feeling of "family." He often will still say that someday he'll be married and have a family, and that it will be "the happiest time of my life."

When all is said and done (which is never, thank goodness but as far as I've come), now I can also say—on the other side of the coin—that to me now a small family is still a family—for this, too, is true. We do not have to feel like leftover parts, an amputated group. We have a wholeness of our own, Richard and me, together, and eventually apart.

Our family isn't so small after all. It never was. I just couldn't see that before.

# 15 / Messages from the World

One day, four months after Dick's death, I received a phone call which shocked me and also sent me on a course on which I hadn't planned to go.

A male voice said, "Karen, this is Joe Brent (not right name). I'm Janice's husband. I know you were a friend of hers and I thought you'd want to know . . ."

Oh, no, I thought. I could feel bad news coming, the way we always can when we hear those words. "Yes, what?"

"Janice took her life—she died yesterday."

I could hardly believe those words. Until Dick's death I had never before known anyone who had even attempted suicide. First my husband, and now a friend. I sat down in stunned disbelief.

"What happened?"

"She took an overdose of pills last week—went into a coma and never came out."

Then he told me of the service which would be held for her. They would all be there, Joe and the children—the three teenagers and the younger son, eight years old, the age

Johanna would have been, and like Johanna, a Down's syndrome child. That, ironically, is how Janice and I had met. Our doctor had delivered her child, the first mongoloid baby he had delivered, and one month later delivered Johanna. He had put us in touch. Janice was a writer, already successful, selling to the big magazines. She had come to visit, after Johanna's birth, and we had become friends. Though we didn't see each other often, we had lunches and talks on the phone. She had shared with me her work and concerns for retarded children and we shared our interest in writing.

She had written a beautiful note to me after Dick's death:

Seemingly there have been too many things to mourn in your young life. May you be comforted.

Please call if there is anything I can do.

The note sat propped by the phone, because I had liked the illustration on the cover so much. It was Verrocchio's "Study for an Angel's Head."

I hadn't called her.

Now I felt a chilly numbness run up and down me—and a shivery rage—God, I thought, what is happening? And then I realized what I had to do. I had to do it now for Dick—and for Janice too—and for all the Dicks and Janices and all the people they left behind. I had to write about it. I hadn't thought I would, but all I could think now was, My God, it happens—it keeps happening—and no one says anything about it. I felt I could. I don't know why I felt that so strongly, but the feeling went clear through me. I had to do it for everybody—for the family of man. Someone had to break the silence.

That night I met with my writing class. Halfway through the evening I realized I had to tell them what had happened. I didn't feel real or present unless I did. I needed to tell them what was on my mind, and so I relayed to them the phone call, and with that story of course I had to include the story of Dick and of his suicide. No one had known before. The students began to talk of their own griefs and losses. They shared and came together after that in a way they never had before.

When I came home I wrote, though in a rather abstract way, about how we don't take the word seriously—"Kids order a drink (all flavors in one) called 'suicide'—'Could I have a suicide please?'"—and "Poets sometimes glorify it. It becomes an easy word to say," I said. Then I told briefly about Dick's choice and about the questions and finally about the choice left to us, the survivors. I felt strongly we had the option and obligation to turn toward the light, and choose life, just as our mate, friend, child or parent chose death. And I guess that maybe even because Dick chose death, I had to make a stand for life. I felt when I wrote it that I was lighting a candle, balancing the darkness, that I had to bring light, and put it in the world for all to see. Doing this was itself an act of survival. I wanted to believe in that light too. If I showed it and other people believed in it, then I could believe in it even more.

I thought I might just send what I had written to a local newspaper. Then I thought of *Newsweek*. I read it and was aware of the "My Turn" column. I decided there was nothing to lose by sending it to *Newsweek*. If they didn't want it, they would send it back. And so I mailed it, just on that whim.

Two days later the phone rang. It was Judy Gingold, an editor at *Newsweek*. "We like your piece," she said, "and are interested in printing it, but I would like to ask something of you. I know it will be painful, so if you don't, I'll understand, but could you be more personal? Tell more of the details and what you went through? I can't even promise then that we'll print it for sure, but I can tell you we are very interested. And if you do write it, would you send it to me express mail so that I get it as soon as possible?"

And so, because now there seemed to be a reason, I was able to once again sit down, pick up pen, and this time go deeper into the pain.

After I wrote and mailed it, a few days passed and a phone call came—they wanted it! I felt thrilled and I felt also it was somehow meant to be—felt in some ways I had very little to do with it. It had happened so easily, as if the world was waiting for it. Within ten days or so, it was on the newsstands.

When I opened *Newsweek* and saw my words there on the page, I felt it had been accomplished—the darkness was balanced.

152

Then the world began to take on a slightly different color. The phone began to ring—calls from all over the United States, amazing calls. In some ways I didn't know what to say, and in other ways I knew it didn't matter what I said. It was the contact that was important. A young law student from Portland just called to tell me he was touched, wished Richard and me well; a woman whose son had just committed suicide called—she only wanted to be able to talk to someone who had experienced a similar loss; a young woman from Los Angeles who lost her first husband in the identical way that Dick had died called, just wanted to tell me she has remarried and is now expecting a baby by her second husband. She wanted to give me hope that there is good life ahead. It was the first time I had contact with anyone who had had a similar experience. And letters—every day—eight, nine, ten, one day nineteen letters, and later a package of copies of letters from *Newsweek*—letters to the editor regarding my story. I felt overwhelmed. I remembered a line from Emily Dickinson—"This is my letter to the world, that never wrote to me . . ." The world had definitely answered my letter. I felt in community with everyone. I didn't read completely all of the letters at that time. Each was so intense and powerful. It was as if I could only take in so much. But I knew this was only a smattering of the people who were affected. I felt a sense of awe and a great sense of humility and responsibility too. We aren't alone. We are all connected by threads of our emotions—our joys and sorrows are one. I knew that through those letters. I had letters from priests, from doctors, from a man in prison. I had letters from husbands who had lost their wives through suicide, from wives who had lost their husbands, from children (now grown) who had lost a parent, and from parents who had lost a son or daughter. I had letters from those others who simply cared and wanted to reach out to us.

Besides the feeling of communion, when anyone said my article helped them, that helped balance the guilt I felt.

I had always thought if I ever wrote or did anything that caused me to receive letters, I would answer all. But so far I have only answered a few. This book, I feel, is in a sense my return gift.

As I began this chapter in the book, I wanted to share a few

153

lines from letters, and so I began to reread some, and read for the first time the ones I had skipped over. I became very emotionally involved in the letters—the letters I had put off, put away in manila envelopes. I unfolded each, one by one, and as I read, tears came to my eyes. A mother told me of her son's death by car accident at eighteen, and then of her daughter's suicide at that same age. "It is hard to go on," she said. I rummaged through my desk for paper, and I wrote her. How could I have not responded earlier? I thought. Almost a year had gone by. Yet I realized that earlier I wouldn't have been able to hear her pain, or to receive, too, her gift of sharing. It was then all too much for me. Each letter was a world in itself—each a soul on paper. I had received a precious treasure, and I had a responsibility, too, I felt, in those manila envelopes.

Some were typed neatly, some scribbled hurriedly:

"Having endured and survived a similar experience, I read [your essay] with keen interest and compassion . . ."

"I have been down the route your husband went in my thinking many times."

"What your husband came to is something I have thought of doing many times, and recently the drive has been special and acute. It is not as though I sit down and contemplate the act, but rather that the act sits down and decides to take over my consciousness."

"It will be four years since the day when my mother committed suicide . . . never in my wildest dreams could my father, brother, or I fathom such an act."

"Your current article . . . prompted a mental return to 1967 when I was at the same point as [your husband] . . . I have asked myself many times since then, 'What made the difference between life and death?'"

"Often times I have the same feelings that your husband did, and I'm sure my wife is as lost as you are."

"I'm sure you wrote the article for me as well as for yourself."

A Franciscan friar wrote: "When I read your story I felt sorry for you because the death that touched you was special. I can imagine the questions and guilt that must have entered your heart."

"My son took an overdose of drugs. . . . I believe I began to heal when I realized that to be human is to be imperfect, to fail those we love. . . . It is better to forgive ourselves. . . ."

"My husband too took his life for reasons he attributed to work-related stress he could no longer bear. He shot himself two weeks before he would have completed a residency in obstetrics and gynecology. . . ."

"I have multiple sclerosis . . . none of us are strangers to anguish."

"I am a trash hauler. A few days ago while working I picked up this magazine . . ."

"Sixty-one years ago, I was an orphan living in a foster home in a little village in northern Wales . . . We had finished a meal of buttermilk and potatoes, and for some reason my foster mother looked at me and said, 'You must be told how your father died before you get the story from someone else. He committed suicide.'"

"I'm not sure yet I have really accepted my husband's death as self-inflicted. The police reports were conclusive, and so is the coroner's. My sons know it too. When will I?"

"Our son committed suicide eight years ago. I am sharing your grief even though we are strangers. . . . In time you find just a corner of your heart always a bit heavy."

From a woman whose husband also committed suicide:

155

"When my family or friends remark how well I am doing I always answer, 'There's no choice.'"

I learned from the letters that others who lost someone through suicide sought grief groups and were mostly turned away or disappointed. They sought a group to understand their particular plight, and there were none. Often they were told, "The only one who can help you is someone else who has been through it."

I did not find this to be true. The people who helped me were people who supported life, people who seemed to like me as a person, people who accepted me, and people who gave me love, and that I could love or appreciate.

As I reread the letters I found myself answering many of them—feeling touched by many. Now I could see them more clearly—more individually.

I felt touched, loved, and at the same time felt a resistance to having lengthy contact with others who have suffered a similar loss. We know we are there, but the sameness isn't in those events. There is sameness or oneness, but it is in our essence—all people's essences. The events just brought us together. The sameness is in our ability to love, to learn, to cry, touch, feel, create, and to let go. Suicide is only a surface event. Surviving is also a surface event. They are acts and roles we engage in. We live and we die, and we try to touch ourselves and others in between. There is a connection, but I feel it more through our strengths than through our weaknesses. More through our wholeness than through our wounds.

There were many letters offering religious consolation—and letters asking to know of help available.

One woman simply sent these lines from a poem by Edna St. Vincent Millay:

> Life must go on,
> And the dead be forgotten;
> Life must go on,
> Though good men die;
> Anne, eat your breakfast;
> Dan, take your medicine;

> Life must go on;
> I forget just why.

A woman whose husband committed suicide eight years ago wrote:

> There was a large memorial service to which many people came, and they all told me what a wonderful man he was (which I knew anyway), and some of them said, "Of course, he couldn't help it," (true), and some said, "Of course it wasn't my fault either" (true, but not very sustaining), but no one has ever, to this day, uttered the words I ached to hear: "You made him happy. . . ."

> Over the years I have realized that those words I longed to hear were true. I have had to say them to myself in the mirror . . . but I am now trying to say them out loud to our four children, who were strongly affected by his death.

> Here, for all those who still "don't know what to say" is a message which will at least partially comfort those who must survive such a loss:

> Think back to all the wonderful times you had. Remember when you both laughed. Remember when he looked at you and smiled. Remember when he called to you. Remember that he chose you.

> Tell your son in detail how much his father enjoyed his existence, how proud he was of his first steps, first words, report cards, etc.

> All of those happy times existed and will remain forever, and nothing can take them away—not even the disease of suicide. You did make him happy.

> And if a disease of despair cast a temporary shadow on his mind, so that he could not see the happiness that was

there, this doesn't mean that the conditions for happiness never existed.

To all those who wrote and shared with me I want to say now how much I appreciated each thought. Thank you.

One of the calls that came soon after the article appeared was from a national television station. They wanted me to appear on a talk show. They would fly me and Richard to Los Angeles, put us up overnight. I said yes. It seemed it was an extension of my article, and appropriate.

Richard and I flew to Los Angeles and were picked up in a limousine at the airport. Richard took pictures of the limo from every possible angle, while the driver stood by and tried to keep a straight face. He'd probably never driven any people quite like us before. This trip was an ironic mixture of some serious business, and of a fantasy world we'd never known before.

The interview went well. I did not meet the woman hostessing the show until our on-air interview, but her interest and warmth felt genuine to me. She shared with me, too, during a break, that she had lost someone in the mass suicide in Guyana, which was also November of '78—the NBC cameraman who was shot with Congressman Ryan was her dear friend. So there was rapport when we talked.

Once my interview was over, a well-known psychiatrist-author was interviewed the second half. I was in the control booth watching, and suddenly I couldn't believe what I was seeing and hearing. He was discussing my situation—talking about Dick, referring to him as "this man," referring to me as "this woman." He made judgments, pronouncements, analyzed the situation and diagnosed it . . . said I was denying my anger. It was as if I had been an example for his "case in point."

I said, "I can't believe this," and the other people in the booth also shook their heads. One man said, "I can't either. I think you should say something about it." Once the interview was over I went to the hostess and the director.

"If he wants to see my anger, I have some now—and it's for him," I said.

"Oh, listen," the director said, "don't pay any attention to

158

that—you were great. That is what people will remember."

Then they handed me the flowers that had been on the set and the hostess gave me her phone number to call and talk if I wanted to after I saw the show on TV later that night.

The limo driver took us back to the motel, pointing out the sights of Hollywood as we passed them.

Back in the room, Richard soon went to sleep. It was late. He was tired. Then the loneliness set in. Here I was—I'd had an article in *Newsweek*. I'd just been on national television. I'd had letters from all over—I'd probably get more now, but there was no one to be with me. It seemed very ironic. I knew a lot of people might have wanted what I had right then, without the strange, sad circumstances that had brought me there. I'd had a tiny taste of a life some people struggled for, and yet I knew from the taste, the emptiness of it. The thing I had always wanted was to love and be loved. I had wanted the feminine dream—never wanted to be a success (not that this could be called "success"). And yet, even with its emptiness, this experience was a glimmer of purposeful work. In some ways I couldn't shake the feeling that there were lots of people out there who responded in some way to an experience like ours, and that was important. And I felt in some ways that Dick was with me. I was doing this, after all, as an extension of our life together.

I tried to think if I had any friends in Los Angeles. I remembered David Black, a musician friend of my brother's who now lived in Hollywood and who was now an arranger and coordinator for several well-known singers. I called Dave, and the talk we had gave me contact, not only with him, but with earth, with myself. It somehow grounded me. Contact with another human being, not one-way contact with millions, was something I needed.

Soon the show was aired. As I watched it I still felt offended by the comments made by the psychiatrist during the second half. I worried that I had perhaps harmed Dick's memory by exposing him, but I knew too there was nothing I could do now. I tried to push it away—let it go. When we returned home, though, I discovered my friends in the philosophy department were all angry about the second half of the show.

159

They felt amazed, said it was inappropriate and wrong for me to have been discussed that way. At least then I knew it wasn't my imagination. But I let it go on by me, because it was, in fact, over. It is one of the risks we take when we expose ourselves to the media, however unfair it may seem.

The experience had its effect, though. It caused me to feel very cautious when another invitation to appear on television came in the mail one day. This was from a St. Louis station. The producer of a public information program in St. Louis, called "ActionLine," wanted me to appear. Besides the caution, a part of me also felt—Maybe this is enough of that sort of thing. Richard even said, "Oh, Mom, didn't you do enough? You wrote that article. You were on one TV show. Now why do you have to be on another?"

I felt very ambivalent about going, but the producer was so positive, so encouraging, and though I said "no" at several points, I finally said, OK. It is amazing to realize we don't always know what good may be in store, because this trip and this experience gave me a happy memory and special new friends for Richard and for me, too, and we both needed that.

But first there was the trip to Oklahoma. I had planned that—wanted it for me and for Richard together.

# 16 / Back in Time

*Chopping Vegetables*

The chopping that I hear
in the kitchen,

It is my mother
          chopping,
          chopping carrots for the night,
          onions, cabbage,
          carefully,
          precisely,
like I too chop
away the people who would threaten
                              or enclose.

Carefully, precisely
only one way to do it.
Less painful they say
          than tearing,
          shredding.

161

Chop, chop,
  cleanly the steel knife
  on the pocked wooden board.


We cut off
  or we are cut off.
  It goes on.


Strong and sure, without hesitation,
the chopping, chopping continues
in a kind of meditative rhythm.
You can let it be your heartbeat.
It begins to sound like home.
Soon we will make soup.

(previously
published in
*Citybender,* Vol. II, No. 5,
and in *Voices on the Last Frontier,*
Windansea Press)

There are many ways not only of connecting with our past, but of then cutting some of the cords.

The first summer after Dick's death I felt a strong urge to return to the place of my birth and to see my few remaining relatives, and for Richard to know where I'd come from, and to meet a few of his relatives too. It seemed important then. There was in me a feeling of wanting to touch base—to go back to "go" again, and start another journey.

My own mother had taken my brother and me, then eleven and thirteen, from Oklahoma all those years ago when she was just exactly my age, forty. She and my dad had just been divorced, after years of problems, and she wanted us to pick up our lives and move to California, "the promised land."

I still remember the way I felt the night we left, as I looked out the train window.

I saw my relatives all standing there on the red time-worn bricks, and I felt a hurting inside—an irreversible sadness, fear, feeling of loss. We were leaving. We were really leaving everything I knew. The whistle of the train cut through, severing all bonds. I felt the tears come, and I saw my grandmother, her prim little smile and her soft brown eyes, trying to look a little encouraging. My blind grandfather saw us leave as surely as anyone else, and I will always remember him, standing so mountainlike. He was the stable head of the family. My uncles and aunts all waved slowly.

As the train pulled away that night I saw the white smoke of that train enclose them like a dream that was ending.

The sound of the rushing train took over, and we were going, cutting through the night and out of the little town before there was time to take a second look back.

I tried to blink back tears. It has always been hard for me to leave.

Now, twenty-seven years later, my own life changed and set free, Richard and I started on the journey back. But I knew before I started on my journey—there is no paradise, and there is really no going back, but I did feel a desire for escape from what had happened, from the pain of Dick's death. I wanted to feel the burden of pain slowly lift from me as we drove east of town, into the mountains, and away.

The heat became intense, and the driving was a chore, doing it all myself, but on the other hand, life is very simple on a long car trip. I didn't have to worry what I should do with my life on those days. I just drove. At the end of each day was the reward of a motel room, maybe a swimming pool, and a dinner. The task at hand covered many random and painful thoughts in my mind. And all the experiences were fresh.

Journal entry, June 27, 1979:
It is 116° in Phoenix. We ate dinner at the Hyatt—the Compass Room on the top—it revolves. Richard thoroughly enjoyed this. Afterwards we walked to the Plaza. I looked again at the beautiful sculptures ("Dance") and loved them. A hillbilly band was playing as I looked at

163

these very aesthetic creatures—while an Indian boy walked by. Contrasts. This is Phoenix.

We've seen a few vagrants. Richard was concerned. Then he said something very poignant. He said, "You know, the worst thing would not be being poor or old—the worst thing would be being lonely—that nobody would want to talk to you.

One sobering, back-to-reality note sounded in Phoenix. It occurred as we registered in the only high-rise we stayed in on our trip. We were handed a key to a room on the eleventh floor. Richard looked at me and said, "Mom—the eleventh floor." It was that floor Dick had jumped from. We asked for another room.

The next day Flagstaff was beautiful with its pine trees and mountains, and the wonderful Grand Canyon—a pink-and-beige empty ancient sea. Later we drove to Winslow, Arizona, and went to a little trading post that boasted having the first elevator in America. I fantasized living in some of the towns. I felt as if all possibilities were open to me—and they were.
    I needed to at least mentally toy around with them.
    But all my thoughts were not as positive as my conscious ones.

Journal entry, June 30, 1979:
Guilt dreams on trip—one had to do with Dick saying in a mechanical voice that I would be punished, that I could live now because of Richard—but not later.

Another night—a vague dream—can't remember images, etc., but felt I was to blame.

Last night I dreamed it was all a mistake—and that I was going to bring Chris (Dick's mother) to show her and surprise her. In my dream, since I didn't see his body—I could coax myself to believe he still existed—and that the ashes were someone else's.

164

When we came to Albuquerque, I felt an "at homeness." This was the town where Dick and I had met—where we had gone to college and married.

The people in the motel were friendly—the air felt familiar. We walked around Old Town—bought candles, visited art shops, ate at La Placita, an old Albuquerque restaurant with a tree growing through its central room. It all seemed so known, and not as if sixteen years had passed since those college days—those days of keen hope and innocent love.

And Richard seemed to take to the town and surroundings as easily as if he had been there before.

We visited the campus where Dick and I had gone to school. It was different in some ways, the same in other ways. Just the way the sun feels and the dirt looks—the cracks in the pavement can take you back until you feel a lack of time. Dick's fraternity house was now an ROTC building—but down the street, the Newman Center, where we'd been married, still looked exactly the same.

A lot of years had passed since that day when we officially began our life together—when we walked out of that building for the first time as Mr. and Mrs. Kenyon.

The sanctuary was locked, but when I asked to go in—saying I'd been married there years ago—it was opened for Richard and me.

The afternoon light flooded through the large cranberry-colored glass window in back of the altar. Somehow it was not as large and overpowering as I had remembered it. We sat in the front row for a few minutes. There were worn places in the rug where priests, altar boys, other couples had stood throughout the years. I could almost see us in the places where we had stood that day, and I remembered the thirty or so friends and family members gathered to share the day with us.

It occurred to me that if I wanted to remove my wedding ring, this would be an appropriate place. I put my fingers around it, but I couldn't do it yet. I just wasn't ready.

In a few minutes we left—and next morning we were once more on our way.

Once in Oklahoma we stayed with my aunt and uncle in Oklahoma City. We saw cousins, spent time in Guthrie where I had grown up. I drove past the house where my grandmother had lived. I remembered all the times I had walked up the stairs, calling out, "Grandmother, I'm here." It seemed strange to see the same red bricks in front, the familiar screen door, and know she wasn't there anymore.

I remembered with some sadness I could have made a trip back to see her while she was in a rest home, but I had put it off, and now later my uncle had told me how her spirit was broken there—how they had tied her to her bed—just because she had wanted to walk to town.

I drove past the house my parents and brother and I had lived in when I was a small child. I remembered the happy days, sitting on the end of the piano bench while my mother played the piano so magically. I was always spellbound and in love with the music. I think now that perhaps my feeling for poetry came from her music. I remembered my brother and me, as small children, playing in the backyard, the swing on the cottonwood tree, the radish garden behing the big bush, and the way the cotton filaments fell like snow in the summer. And I remembered sitting on the front porch, waiting for my dad to come home from work, counting the cars until I saw ours. Now the house just looked stark white, unfamiliar in a sense—not misty and shrouded in memories, laughter, and fantasy, as it had lived in my mind.


Since I couldn't remember the address I asked my aunt to show me the house where my parents lived when I was born. We drove around the little houses, skirting the town's park. "It was one of these," she said. At first, not sure which of two it was, she finally settled on one. I looked at it—the windows, front door and small porch looked like a face, a face I had a vague sense of knowing. Looking at the small yard I imagined I must have been out there, at least in my buggy. It was hard to make it seem real again, but this was as real as Dick's and my life together—and as out of reach. Only right now, this moment, was real in the sense of being palpable, touchable.

We went back to my aunt's house and Richard later went swimming with my cousin's children—in the pool I had also gone swimming in as a child. I recalled my mother swimming there too. She was one of the few adults in town who would actually go swimming. In Guthrie, Oklahoma, children swim, adults watch. But my mother had been more alive than most, a rebel of sorts, and though her life in California had ended in less than a glorious, happy way, it was important she had tried. She had risked, dared, and by doing so, she had set a new platform for my life and my brother's. She hadn't fit in in this town, and I knew I certainly didn't now either.

Another day we drove past the house my family and I had lived in on the west side of town. Once an amazing tree grew in front—a tree that housed many episodes of Tarzan. I recalled one boy always had the lead role of Tarzan, and another girl and I alternated playing Jane. One day they cut the tree down, as Tarzan, the two Janes, Boy, and Cheetah all sat forlornly on the front porch. This house also had a wonderful playhouse in the backyard—big enough for two cots, a table, and at least fifty comic books, from Donald Duck to Captain Marvel to Wonder Woman. Fantasies and dreams grew there. My dad had built a brick outdoor barbecue back there, and he had written our names and the date in the cement when he finished. I knew it must still be there, but somehow I only wanted to see the front of the house and to remember. Like the tree, all of this existed in my memory anyway.

Once there in Oklahoma I began to feel it wasn't necessary to stay long. It was a pilgrimage back, and I could see nothing of me was there anymore. I was, in a sense, a stranger there. My parents, and the child I used to be, were figments of imagination in the minds of people still living there, and in my mind too. They remembered that child, and now I had outgrown skins of years—heart outgrowing heart, soul dropping layers—until little was left of the little girl I had once been. The only real going home anyway was in my head. I could recall with such clarity the chickens in my grandmother's yard, my dad's ominous, dusty law office, the way my mother smelled, clean and powderey-good when she was dressed to go out. I could remember the pavement—funny how pavement is so important to kids. I wondered why the brick wall around the library was only half as high as in my mind. These memories were

167

inside me. My childhood was in some ways left here, and I used to think I had lost it, but I had it inside me all the time.

There in Oklahoma I experienced many positive recollections of my parents—my parents who had separated before we left, and that I could never put together in my mind. Remembrance by the older people there of my mother's youth, of her piano playing, of her laughter. And there was mention of my father. My uncle, my mother's brother, referred to him as "one of the finest gentlemen I ever knew." My father, whom I had always felt was the villain in the war between my parents, here—twenty-seven years later—seemed vindicated as I was shown other views. I was grateful. I was given the gift of seeing my parents together again through others' eyes, and reminded of their goodness.

I recalled my father's dream of my making a "successful" marriage. I remembered the time, shortly after Dick's and my marriage, when we stopped in Guthrie on our drive across the country. Dick and my father had met. Though my dad had already had a stroke, he was back at his office, dressed in his suit and vest, wanting to be his old self. He seemed to like Dick, and to "approve" of him. This was important to my father. He held family and education in high esteem, and he felt Dick fulfilled what he wanted for me. Would he have sought different values now? I remembered my mother's dream for me to have beautiful babies. I think one of her happiest days was when I had Richard.

It doesn't ever all go together, but a piece here and there do add. It is hard now to separate dreams, to know what mine had been. They had always been changing. I knew that. I had a baby and lost it. I'd had a husband and lost him, at least in this world. But I think my dream inside was still to just find some kind of joy, make some kind of wonderful sense—to touch some purpose within the depths of myself, and touch the depths of a few other human beings. This, I felt, was still possible in this city by the sea, and in my life.

Richard came home thinking he looked like my grandmother's Irish side, the "Mahoneys," because of his reddish hair and freckles. Always before he was a Kenyon and nothing else. And yet, he is only Richard, or what is beneath the name Richard. He is who he is, as I am also, but I suppose I had to go back and dig around, collect and look, in order to set it down this time for myself. Not because my mother left this past of ours, but now because this time, I left it.

We drove to Taos, New Mexico, on the return trip. Here was a true spirit-home for me. I still treasure the feeling of Taos in my heart: the wise storm-blown sky in the afternoon, the breathless spotting of late afternoon's warm rain, the hidden courtyards with bright flowers and yesterday's faded wash, the symmetry of adobe dwellings and stairways. While there we drove to D. H. Lawrence's ranch. The house he lived in for two years was there, and the Lawrence tree, once painted by Georgia O'Keeffe, was in front. Horses were kept to the side, and the grassy meadow was rich and lush and seemed to go on forever. Up a little path was the chapel where his ashes were kept, and a carving of a phoenix bird, an important symbol to Lawrence.

The road to the ranch was long, winding and bumpy. Richard complained, and I apologized to the car often, but this part of the trip seemed to connect me back to the feeling of "artist" within me.

The Taos pueblo was like a moment out of time and space. Smoke rising from the bread ovens, the fresh stream running through the center of the pueblo where Indians still collect drinking water in buckets each day. I felt a tranquility there that put my heart at peace. In my mind I still sit near it.

We stopped in Albuquerque overnight on the return trip, but I still wasn't ready to remove my wedding ring, though soon I would—in an uneventful, almost "trying it out" way.

The desert drive was hot. Phoenix was again unbearable. We spent all afternoon in an air-conditioned shopping mall, and then in early evening, when the temperature had dropped to 107 degrees, started to drive home. I drove until early morning. We passed finally through the large shadowy mountains that let us know we were coming back into the southern

California we knew—and we finally arrived home.

And it was good to be back. I didn't feel I wanted to be away again for a while, and I didn't need to go back anymore, at least not in the immediate future. San Diego was "home."

Part of the going back was to realize there really wasn't any part of me back there. The promised land is really inside. I had wanted to see what I had left behind, what I'd missed, but what I had missed was not my life there. I had no life there. My life was always where I was. My past was inside me, and so was my future.

The trip was all part of cutting cords from my early life. There was an aspect of my college life that needed to be cut off, and when it surfaced, I cut another cord.

In college I had been an art major, and so I could express myself and live in my world of creativity, but the other side of me had to conform to the reality of society. I belonged to a sorority—not because I wanted to, but because my father had told me I had to, or not go to college. I had worked for two years after high school, and I wanted that chance to go to school to learn and perhaps be more. The actuality of what a sorority really meant came into clear focus a few months after this trip. It was as if in my new life I had new eyes, and I could see the cords that needed to be cut, could see situations I had gone along with mindlessly—things I hadn't chosen. I realized how utterly I am against what sororities and fraternities stand for—exclusivity, separation. I realized (after all those years) there are no black girls, no Chinese girls, no Jewish girls in sororities. I'm told there are a few nowadays, but the whole idea of these elite clubs is alien to me. I believe in togetherness, not separation.

I realized how usually I am not even aware of someone's creed or religion—or background. I began to feel terribly ashamed that I could have even been a silent conspirator— even been a party to a group which would choose its members because of race, creed, color, and dollars. I decided I needed to take a stand, however late it might be, and however trite it might seem at this point. I wrote my sorority, though it had been all those years. I said I didn't want any longer to have my

170

name associated with them. And I said, "That doesn't mean I don't still care for some of the friends I still have from those days—but I don't want anyone thinking I approve of the organization." It is a small thing, but I felt it needed to be done.

I had worked twenty hours a week while in college, so I didn't just have everything handed to me, but I didn't want any longer to give a silent consent to any kind of prejudice. By my mother's leaving Oklahoma, she had cut that cord. I guess I wanted to live out my legacy, and also what was truly inside me.

Other cords were either cut by now, or soon would be.

With friendships and family, it had been clear, some people had cut themselves off, but new flowers had grown in their places.

Quitting my job at UCSD was an important cord to cut—from dependence on a schedule, certain security, and from the strong association of Dick having worked and died there. How could I work for an institution he had told me, in his note, had "killed" him?

The entire trip to Oklahoma was a release from the past—another snip, and old blooms dropped away, and yet the people who were still there and who mattered to me were seen anew.

As the cords were cut and the new tielines made to the present and future, so, too, old wounds could be healed and re-bound. The other aspect of going back is to reconnect, and sometimes that can best be done in our minds, for there are many ways to go back.

One evening I was invited by a friend to a conference where Ruth Carter Stapleton was one of the speakers. Her quiet, direct manner was touching, and the meditation she led gave me something I had been missing. The meditation caused us, each one, to re-experience ourselves as little children, in our homes with our parents. She calls this process, "inner healing." I remembered the house where my parents had lived when I was born. She said, "Picture Jesus coming in and picking you up." Though I don't normally picture Jesus in my mind, I did this. "Now," she said, "He holds you, and shows you love, heals

171

your hurts . . . and now your mother comes in. You look in your mother's eyes, and see her hurt. You know you carry those wounds now." I could feel the emotion in me, though I tried to suppress it, could see my mother had given me all she had to give me—which was a lot—but most important, I could see her needs, her own unmet needs, the love she herself had received, which hadn't been enough. Could I bind that wound now? Bridge that gap between my mother and me? Then she said, "Now your father comes in, and you see his eyes, and you say, "Daddy, it is OK that you weren't perfect." What an incredible thing to say. I could see my father's brown eyes, and I knew they held love. Maybe I just never saw that, but I could feel it now.

There was a binding of love between us all during this meditation. It erased time and space. The emotions, and the inner mother and father, were all present and viable, and right then the experience was felt as release—of love—and as a connection and a sinking into love. Even though I couldn't totally allow myself to go into the depth of the feelings, I tapped into them and could see the importance of being rebound to my parents. In our parents' love is the seed of our beginning. As Paul Brenner has stated so beautifully in his book, *Life Is A Shared Creation* (De Vorss & Company, Publisher), "Love, as well as the genetic code, has the power to be transmitted through each dividing cell of the unfolding embryo."

We can perhaps go back and bridge the gaps with our parents, as Ruth had suggested in the meditation. And if we can bridge it with our parents, then, I thought, I can also bridge it, inside myself, with Dick, and maybe Richard can too, someday. All is not lost.

I wished so much Dick could have experienced a bonding with his own parents, and still I think perhaps this, too, is still possible, at least through them. I had never facilitated or encouraged closeness with his family, and that I believe was a serious mistake I made. Somehow we had both wanted to always be so separate and independent. But are we ever separate and independent? And do we even really want to be? Aren't we always part of where we've been—whether we like it

172

or not, whether it is painful or not—and part of all who've loved us and that we've loved? Most especially we must be connected still to that moment of our conception when we came from two different worlds, and became a wholeness forged of opposites.

I have tried to remember, somewhere in the depths of my mind—and soul—how it was . . .

There must have been passion between my parents during my conception—there must have been hope—but was there love? I believe there was, but I also believe it was masked love, because I never saw my parents outwardly showing or expressing affection or love—and still I know it had to be there, or they wouldn't have been drawn together. They were drawn in love, love that was afraid to show its face—to expose itself. Is that why I try so hard to show the face of my own love, and still have a hard time doing that—and show it mostly on paper, or at a distance?

This sort of thought process is very much a part of Paul Brenner's book, and I feel it is essential to explore in order to truly live, and I suppose that when we've had to let go—when some of our life has died—and we are ready to be reborn in a sense, maybe we do have to go back, and recall how it was the first time around.

And how was my birth? The year was 1938—a hospital in Oklahoma City.

I think I perhaps liked it in the womb, up to a point, and then it was time to go—and as the contractions began, I felt excited. It was natural and right to leave, and even though my world was tumultuous at that point, it was something I had to go through, and I wanted to be born. I was anxious to be born. But the labor went on—and on—and progress wasn't made. The tumult became tiring. I even began to feel panicked—would I ever get out of there? My mother was in pain. I could feel that. She began to resent me because of the pain, and yet she wanted me very much, but during this time she hurt too much to love anymore, only wanted everything to be over. Three days, and she grew weak.

It was decided—Caesarian was the only way.

173

The sedative took. My world quieted . . . and just as I had given up hope—the world opened above me. I was lifted up into the light by kind strong hands, gentle blue eyes gazed on me, and a masked face was haloed by overhead light.

And I began to breathe.

I know my mother did not breast feed me—that she tried, but the anesthetic had affected her milk. I know she was totally pleased and thrilled with me—I was a pretty baby in her eyes. I was formed well—my head not distorted by a normal birth process. This seemed important to her. I had been lifted free without going through the final test.

I know too she never forgot the pain.

And I recall I always thought everyone was born the way I was born, and my brother was born one and one-half years later. I had seen the scar often enough. I knew where I came from. When I finally learned at age eight or nine how other babies were born, I was amazed and felt incredulous—and a bit disgusted. I remember saying, "You mean, just like animals?" I had thought somehow we humans were a different and special species.

This time I've had to push my own way through the birth canal. There's no one there to lift me free, and yet they are there, those who wait to applaud and assist—we're never, ever born totally alone.

Going back, binding and releasing, seemed to give me a feeling of completeness about myself—not something I needed to dwell on, or re-experience anymore, but just to consciously know it.

Going back is part of going on.

> We shall not cease from exploration
> And the end of all our exploring
> Will be to arrive where we started
> And know the place for the first time.

T. S. Eliot, from
"Little Gidding," in
*Four Quartets*

174

# 17 / What Now?

After the trip to Oklahoma, I accepted the invitation to come to St. Louis for the TV show. In many ways I felt directionless, but I was open to possibilities. And I felt, too, in some strange way this was my work. I needed to do this. I couldn't turn my back. The event that had happened was too big for me to just go on my way and try to build my life. I felt something had to be done first, something had to be built from the raw material of the event, and life seemed to be pointing me in that direction, and opening doors for me on a path I needed to follow.

The trip started on an uncertain note: We arrived at the airport and were told at first we had no reservations. Then later we were told we did have them, but they weren't paid for. We were close to flight time, and were told by the reservations clerk that he would check, but that all lines were busy, and probably we wouldn't make this flight. I called Jan Landis, the producer in St. Louis. If we missed this flight, we would miss the show. I started to feel ambivalent about going again. Maybe this was all wrong. But once Jan had the information, she made calls. Miraculously it was all settled just minutes before flight time. The trip went fine, and once there I knew almost immediately the decision to come was right.

Everything felt in tune. When we arrived in St. Louis we were met by a blonde, pretty, smiling woman. It was Jan. And by Jan's assistant, Becky—bubbly and welcoming. From the minute we met them, the very air felt good. They treated us both like long-lost relatives. Richard was totally charmed, and took to them immediately. They drove us through the city to the hotel, pointing out the sights.

Once in the hotel, Jan went to the desk to get the room key. We all got on the elevator, and I saw her push floor eleven. I almost gasped, but didn't say anything, and yet I felt panic and uneasiness inside. When we walked to the room and entered, we discovered it was still unmade and not ready for us. I said to Jan, "Could we just change the room anyway?" And then I reluctantly explained to her why.

I hated to say it, but somehow felt I needed to. Jan and Becky both apologized for the room, and said, "Of course."

Once we were situated in the new room, they left us for a few hours. We changed, unpacked, and looked around the hotel. Later Becky picked us up for the show. She called up to the room a little early, "This is Becky—I wanted to drive you around and show you the 'Arch' and the waterfront and the old railroad station—so whenever you're ready we can just go." There was friendliness here that went beyond bare necessity.


Once at the studio I was interviewed in front of an audience. They were all interested and concerned. Some were social workers. Others, I suspected from their questions, had experienced a suicide in their own family.

A woman came up to me later and asked if I were traveling around the country to talk to groups. She said that if I would, she felt it would be wonderful.

But, I thought, that isn't me—is it? I felt torn. What should I do? That wasn't my way. What was my way? Dick's death seemed to call for something beyond just rebuilding my life—

176

and yet how much? Or is this kind of thing part of rebuilding my life?

Jan, Becky, and Jan's husband, Gary Polovich, treated us warmly, took us out to an old St. Louis night spot for dinner. The next evening was saved for a ball game—the St. Louis Cardinals, something Richard would like. It is perhaps hard to realize how much all of this meant to us. When you've lost— perhaps the slightest injustice is magnified, but also kindnesses are so wonderful, so incredibly appreciated. You just want to cry for kindnesses.

The next day Richard and I rode on a riverboat down the Mississippi. I remembered St. Louis was the place my mother had always spoken of—the one big trip she had taken with friends as a young working girl, to a big world's fair here. Richard later rode to the top of the great arch. I recalled that Dick and I had driven by here on our trip across the country when we were first married. They were just beginning to build it at the time.

Later that evening Gary came to the hotel to take Richard to the ball game. When they came back Richard was high and happy, and with a new close friend.

The next day, Jan and Gary both took us to the airport and we left for San Diego. Richard told me later, "You know, Mom, I've hardly ever felt sad about leaving anyone, but I felt all teary when we had to leave Jan and Gary. I really want to see them again. People always say 'We'll see you again' but most of the time you don't, and I really want to see them again." He had felt strong love for them both, and perhaps just because he had given it and felt it so freely, it was reciprocated. We've kept in touch, and we did stop to see them again several months later on a Thanksgiving trip to visit Dick's parents in Florida.

Richard's heart may have been wounded by the loss of his father, but this incident showed clearly he was very much able to love. And for me, it was really one of the first positive happy experiences—something that was ours alone—part of our new life.

Journal entry, August 8, 1979:
St. Louis was wonderful. The best experience Richard and

I have had in our new life. Jan, Gary and Becky—all super people—positive, happy, bubbly, bright. It was energizing to be around them. They couldn't have been nicer.

The difference right now—because of St. Louis—is that I think Richard and I are both beginning to live our own lives more. I know it gave me more of a sense of self. Life is still here.

Once home I busied myself with an occasional article. My summer school class didn't have enough students, so there were weeks before teaching began again. I gave myself over to entertaining Richard. I took him and his friends fishing off the Shelter Island Pier many early mornings.

Journal entry, August 10, 1979:
. . . it's pretty, peaceful and fresh in the A.M. by the water.
I drink coffee and read—and they have lots of fun. Today they caught five fish—and ate four for lunch!

I took Richard to play miniature golf one night. He said, "I'll go, but it won't be fun. It was fun with Dad because he was good, but you can't even hit the ball—and so it takes the fun out of it." Strangely enough, though, as we played I not only hit the ball, but I also made several holes-in-one. I didn't even think about it. It would just happen. Each time I only realized what I had done once the ball was hit. I had an awed sensation, and yet I feared saying anything about it—almost afraid to break the spell.
Then as we got in the car to drive home, I just started to cry. I felt a longing for Dick. I missed him. It wasn't the sadness of feeling his pain. It wasn't the sadness of feeling sorry for myself. I just had such a strong feeling that he was there at the golf course. The feeling was so real that I truly missed his presence then as we drove.
During these months I began to have a very strong feeling that I didn't want to "blow" this time in my life and Richard's— that I wanted, no matter how uncomfortable it might be, to really take time, let things be, not rush into jobs, relationships,

178

busyness. I began to feel like a seashell—empty, clean, waiting.

Journal entry, August 12, 1979:
Tonight I read a little in an old notebook, written around the time Johanna died. I can see more clearly now what was going on. I rushed into myself, into other people and activities, into questioning, etc., to escape the birth and loss of our baby. It depressed me to read it.

Though I didn't realize it, I was making a decision to let myself empty out—to not have to fill in all the spaces—to be patient and learn to wait—to leave spaces for purpose and love and hope.

The house was also very much in order at this point. The poster of a seashell by Georgia O'Keeffe hung over the fireplace, and seemed to say it all.

It was during this time I did remove my wedding and engagement rings. Not with a big ceremony. I took them off one day, and I think I wore them again a day or two later, then took them off again. It began to feel natural not to wear them.

At this point though, all I really hoped for was to keep making it through. One thing I was sure of—something in me felt very wrong about cluttering myself so that I couldn't feel and experience everything. I wanted to keep in touch with "knowing" and I was beginning to have a sense of that. I realized experience does not necessarily teach us, but that being aware of our experience can.

Journal entry, August 13, 1979:
Can someone be scarred like this—and still come out whole?

Journal entry, August 18, 1979:
I have to make something in my new life. I have been left on a desert island with a few tools. What will I make for myself? And for Richard?

Journal entry, September 12, 1979:
I want to try more to face myself. I have to stop running. I

have to face my nothingness—my void. What do I have to be afraid of? I want to continue to reach out—but to also begin to sink into myself more. . . .

During this time I began to meditate, and to take walks on the beach alone. It felt good to touch base with myself and with some kind of inner knowing, to experience the "empty full-ness."

# 18 / Richard

Richard was named after his father—the first name anyway, but as a young child he always looked very little like Dick. Dick would tease: "Where did this red-haired, freckled-face boy come from?" During his first year or two he looked a lot like some of my baby pictures, but mostly he just looked like Richard, unique, one of a kind. Lately, though, I see Dick's features—his sensitive masculinity revealing itself in Richard. And Richard is starting to identify positively with Dick. He'll say, "I'm good at barbequing, just like Dad was," or "I get a lot of my tastes from Dad, I think—like blueberry muffins and licorice." Several friends have remarked, "I never saw Dick in Richard before, but now I'm beginning to—the gestures, too, the way he stands and moves, and the way he acts—the teasing." At first I didn't want to hear this. It saddened me, but more and more that feeling has become one of appreciation. Richard is part of Dick, as he is part of me, but most of all, he is himself.

It's not easy when a child loses a parent, and it is especially hard when the parent takes his own life, and yet loss itself was

181

not new to Richard. He had already lost an adopted baby sister he'd known for six weeks, a baby sister he'd known for six months, and later some hope for another brother or sister.

Though he wasn't at all sure why his dad had done what he did, he knew what things *weren't* the cause. In the early days when I felt guilt and would say, "Oh, I should have done this . . . or I should have done that . . ." Richard would say, "Mom, that is not why he did it."

I had explained to him once that it was maybe like a sickness—that Dad had been dying only we just didn't know he was sick. I didn't really know what was true, but that seemed close, and Richard accepted that. He knew Dick's final act had nothing to do with the kind of father he had been, or anything he or I had done, or not done. It was something beyond all of that.

When Johanna had died, Richard had buried a doll in place of Johanna, and the reality was that he had missed playing with his sister. Now he had another, even greater loss to assimilate.

He told me once that when I told him about Dick's death, he at first felt a wave of sadness, and then anger came in, and he felt mad. And this to me sounds so normal. How else could he feel? How else can a twelve year old accept that kind of loss, or can any of us? Richard's emotions have always been clear and appropriate too, not full of "shoulds." A few days later he said to me, "You know, Mom, this is probably harder on me than it is on you, because Dad and I used to do so many things together. I'll never have another father, but maybe you'll have another husband." Of course the truth is you never, ever, replace a human being, but the fact that he could say anything that vulnerable still amazes me. I could barely reply to that, let alone say it.

During those first few months, Richard seemed to say all the truths we could have known at the time. From the beginning, that is, after the end, Richard's secret wisdom always seemed to be present. His words were never many, but when he said something you knew he had integrated his loss and that it had worked its power on him. Richard could say words I wouldn't have been able to say, for I couldn't face that kind of pain, and yet he didn't dwell on it. He said once, "You know Dad just always wanted to protect us so much. That is why he kept so much inside." Those were words I also knew, but I couldn't have given voice to the thought. He also once said, "I think Dad didn't tell us how unhappy he was because he didn't want to bother us. He shouldn't have done that—but you know that is the way he was." And then we talked about the fact that we should always tell each other—that is what being a family means. He also said, "We don't want to get depressed like Dad did. We should live and be happy—and just feel bad sometimes."

Another day as we were driving in the car, Richard said what I think is probably the most incredible thing he has said. "Mom," he looked at me, "let's you and me make a pact right now that we'll never do what Dad did." And so we shook on that. It was our insurance and our bond—our life pact.

Now Richard has good friends. He does well in school and in sports. He loves music, plays trumpet in the band. In a way those losses he's known have forged him in a way few children have experienced. He is wise beyond his years, and yet a typical young boy. All his life, his losses will be part of him, but his wisdom, his survival techniques, will be there too. However he has assimilated his pain inside, he has, as much as possible, assimilated it. And yet I know too the mystery will always play through him.

The relationship Richard had with the therapist for a while helped him through several stages. This doctor helped Richard make the transition from the shock of his father's death to his own continuing life. He also saw clearly through some of the "macho" behavior Richard occasionally indulged in, and his identification for a short time with his uncle, Tom, who likes guns and has a buck's head over the fireplace. The doctor said, "Occasionally, 'macho' behavior is a way of coping. His father was a gentle man, and Richard knows now it didn't work very well. Later, he'll be able to identify with those traits more."

Richard's school helped greatly. The principal and teachers were aware of what happened, and they gave him support, especially the counselor, Betty Quayle. She had also lost a parent at around the same age—her mother—and so she truly understood. Richard was allowed to drop in to see her any time during the day, and they would talk, not necessarily directly about what happened, but it was what went between the lines that mattered. One day she told me, "You know, Richard came in today and told me he had a stomachache. Then she said, with emotion in her eyes, "It's easier sometimes to say you have an ache in your stomach, than that you have an ache in your heart."

That first baseball season without Dick was a hard time for Richard. He always loved playing in Little League, and it was largely tied up and associated with Dick. He supported Richard totally in that—practiced with him, cheered loudly for him. Dick was one of the most enthusiastic parents at the games, and he always had a great time. Richard knew he had one true fan.

Soon after Dick died, Richard said, "Who'll practice ball with me now?" He was realizing the reality of his loss. It's the seemingly little things we miss, and then we realize those things aren't little—they are the fabric of our lives every day. It's the little talks, the walks, the tossing of a ball—that's what life is.

I did a kind of daring thing at that point. I wrote a note to Dave Winfield, then San Diego Padres' baseball star, and told him Richard's predicament—though I had no real expectation of a reply. One night the phone rang, and a voice said, "Mrs. Kenyon, this is Dave Winfield." We talked for a few minutes, and he told me about a baseball camp Richard might attend. Then he asked to talk to Richard.

Richard was sitting on the couch watching TV, and I said, "Someone wants to talk to you."

"Who is it?" he started to get up, disinterestedly.

"It's Dave Winfield."

There is no way to describe the surprise and thrill on Richard's face. His mouth dropped open and his face lit up several watts, I'm sure. "It is?" he said. "It is?"

That incident helped give me faith in the essential goodness in the world.

And yet, as time went on, Richard seemed less interested in

baseball. It just wasn't the same without Dick. That was the sport they shared most strongly. Now Richard loves biking. He goes on fifty- or sixty-mile rides with a club or with friends, and has a lot of pride in keeping his bike in good condition. And he has recently discovered surfing.

"Of all the sports I've done," he said, "I think surfing is the one I was really meant to do. It makes me happier than any other ever has."

He has stepped more now into his own life. Though he still likes baseball, letting go of interest in it was like letting go of that part of the past associated with his father.

And of course, since the last of August, 1979, Richard has had his very special gift, his Big Brother.

Journal entry, August 31, 1979:
Today was a *red letter day* for Richard! He has a "Big Brother"!

Steve calls Richard every week, and they spend hours each week just being together, whether it is walking dogs, washing the car, going to a ball game. Richard has a special friend, a man to talk to and share with, someone to be a role model, and just to be there.

Since they've been together I've been able to release Richard a little more. I'd wanted to protect him so much from pain, but I couldn't do that. And I couldn't give him the gift he has now, either—the gift of a special, caring friend, or the gift of his own integrity and wisdom.

Now it seems my son lives in the first room of his future. It's not his father's room. It's not my room. It is the room of hope and faith in his own future. It is a room of life.

A friend recently told me—now one and one-half years after Dick's death, he is amazed to see how much Richard has grown and changed. And it is true. He's not the little boy he seemed to be before. He is half again as big, and seems to be twice as old inside. Sure, he's very much a kid, full of adolescent pranks, energy, interest in girls, in bike-riding, in surfing—but he has a wisdom that is more than age.

He evokes wonder, awe, and a touch of sadness in me at times to know his fantasies of invulnerability have been taken away so soon. The five year old who used to say, "I'll never die. If I do—I'll just fly right back down from Heaven and be here again," now says, at fourteen, "You know we never know if we'll ever see someone the next day. We always assume we will, but there's no guarantee." Then he goes on to say, "Remember how John Wayne said on TV before he died, that a good day to him is any day he wakes up in the morning? Well, I think that is a pretty neat thing to be able to say."

Richard even uses his new logic and wisdom to see how senseless some things we have to learn in school can seem—at least at the time. One day, struggling over chemistry symbols, he said, "Why should I have to learn chemistry symbols? I was born, and someday I'll die, and does it matter that I knew *H* stood for hydrogen?" In a way you really can't beat that logic!

We huddled together very much psychologically in the early days, both of us like hurt children. I think that is normal and necessary. We were all we had, and we both needed security. With time we both, little by little, have grown more separate. I think a mother and child who have shared a loss do have a special bond that goes past age differences.

There's still much closeness, but it is more of a growing and an adjusting, side by side, and yet there is the realization between us that life can and will end. We know this from our very souls, and it has changed us.

Richard and I, mother and son, care about each other, and we have a space of time now to spend together before he goes away to college someday, or perhaps gets married and builds his own life. And that's all people ever have. Losing someone just makes it all so apparent. We are two spheres that touch and share time and space for awhile. I'll try to never let him down, and I've tried to build a feeling of stability that can exist for us and give us room to grow too.

It's not always idyllic. We argue sometimes, but not for long. Making up and working it out always seems more important than whatever the quarrel was about. Our needs bump into each other at times. My frustrations pour out on him at times,

186

and sometimes his wants are something I can't meet, but we also come to terms. One day I wanted him to do some work around the house, and Richard, quite normally, didn't want to do it. I was frustrated and said, "Why can't you help? I feel like I give so much. Half of everything that is mine is yours!" Richard came over and hugged me. "One hundred percent of mine is yours," he said.

We communicate, trite as that sounds, and it is the greatest gift. We share laundry and dinner and washing the dog. Sometimes I get tired of driving him places. Sometimes I *want* to drive him places because I feel purposeless that day, and I still want to hang on to him and be with him. Sometimes I look at him and know I'm the mother, but sometimes I feel that I am like a "motherless child." He is working out his independence every day, and I am working on mine too. It's more of the releasing again, the letting go, the eternal lesson of life—and so far we are making it.

Sometimes on the news there will be a report of a suicide, and it will graphically bring it home to us—bizarre things do happen, unexplainable things happen, and we are both very aware that one happened to us. But then I'll say, "But we're here, Richard. We're making it—we're OK." It's hard sometimes to acknowledge together that it happened, but it is important too.

Richard is my son—my beautiful son that I always wanted to protect, and that I know for certain now I can't. I try to give him my love, and we both live within trust of each other.

More and more he is acquiring male role models and friends too. Besides his young friends, he now has several adult men who like him and spend time with him—taking him fishing or to play basketball, and he has adult women friends too. On his fourteenth birthday I had a party for Richard. I invited his young friends *and* his adult friends. This is one positive aspect of being the child of a single parent. Often there are several adults who are truly friends of that child, and that is kind of wonderful.

Richard went through, and is still going through, his own stages of grief, and loss—different from mine and really unknown to me, for after all, I only see the outer layer. The only show of deep sorrow and tears I saw was on the plane trip home from his uncle Tom's, after that first Christmas. The anger is something Richard was more open about, telling me at one point that one way he handled what happened (and this was quite soon after), was "staying in reality a lot." When I asked what he meant, he replied, "Just concentrating hard on whatever I'm doing—like playing ball, or riding my bike."

His shock and numbness were very evident at the memorial service. He displayed no outward emotion there. It just didn't seem real. I know, too, the fact we never saw Dick's body made the reality more hazy. And too, Richard didn't go on the boat when we took Dick's ashes to sea. I had asked him, but he said he didn't want to go. It must have seemed like just too much.

Later he told me it seemed for a long time that "Dad was just away on a trip, and then after a long time you realize more and more he is not ever going to come back."

Initially I believe one way Richard sought his father was by almost trying to be him. Once he put on Dick's yellow nylon jacket from his diving club, but it was much too big, and he told me to save Dick's good blue seersucker suit, because "I might want to wear it someday." But the interest in Dick's clothing did not last long. It was all a part of saying goodbye.

Richard still has difficulty saying his dad is no longer alive. He often just looks down at the mention of what has happened.

As I've said, he often referred to Dick in the present tense during the first year. When I made a folder about Dick shortly after his death, Richard said, "Why do people always say, 'Dick would have liked that'? Why don't they say, 'He likes that'?" If someone asks him about his dad, and he is forced to say his dad died, he'll often look shocked and afraid of having to explain. On a train trip a year after Dick's death, Richard met a young artist who visited with him most of the trip. Then the artist said to Richard, "What does your dad do anyway? I'll bet you're really spoiled." Richard just looked frozen. He quickly looked at me. He didn't know what to say. I said, "Richard's dad died last year." The artist looked embarrassed, and he said quickly, "Oh, I'm sorry."

Recently, Richard went to a stained glass class. I heard him say to the instructor, "My dad does stained glass—I mean my dad did stained glass," so the reality of this world is slowly being expressed, but those things take time, and when someone is not gone from your heart, how can you say he is gone?

What is acceptance? Perhaps it is the knowledge of the reality of loss, here and now, coupled with the possibility of more—the acceptance of the unknown and the appreciation of what we've had. I don't think it is painting everything black, and yet, it is hard to really feel it is OK. Richard graphically expresses his feelings when he says he doesn't understand why funeral cars are black. "Why shouldn't they be painted with colors and flowers—because you are happy that person was alive?"

Acceptance and understanding touch on us like waves, and often it is a different understanding than we expected. But it is true the waves keep coming, and as long as we keep living and loving, that immersion occurs more and more.

Recently we went to Scripps Aquarium. We had talked of the fact we hadn't gone for a while. It was a gorgeous day—so we went. Richard usually wants to bring friends along on such outings, but he didn't that day.

Scripps Aquarium is part of UCSD, and though it is not on the campus, it is nearby geographically.

As we walked past the tanks of saltwater fish Richard told me he had been there "with Dad," and he told me about going behind the tanks with Dick—that since Dick knew some of the people there he had been able to give Richard an "insider's tour." He had seen how they feed the fish and maintain the tanks. Later as we walked out past other buildings, he said, "I've seen movies in those buildings."

"Oh," I said, "films about the ocean?"

When I said, "I didn't know you did that with Dad—that's something I didn't know," Richard replied, "Well, there are things you don't know about—that Dad and I did together— just like I don't know all about everything you and Dad did together."

Yes, I have to admit, there's much I don't know about my son's world, or anyone's world. His joy has been his own, from babyhood joy of seeing his first bird to recent joys of shooting off a rocket at the beach, or catching his first fish—and his sorrow, too, is his own to work through. I'm glad he has secrets about his dad—his private pleasures and talks, the times they shared—they're all inside Richard now.

Recently Richard said in a clear moment of understanding, "I'll be a different person, since Dad's gone. It's changed my development."

He, Dick, and I will always be linked somewhere in space and time—but Richard, as we all are, is "a child of the universe."

I found that no matter how hard I tried to insulate him, I couldn't do that. He's had to learn some hard lessons for his young years, and all I can do is sort of step back and observe his unfolding and his own flowering with a little bit of awe and a lot of humility.

For Richard, his father's death is perhaps less a dark legacy than it is a bright challenge.

# 19 / Children

The fact that I have Richard still seems like a miracle to me.
Maybe because having a child was just never easy. It also seems
to me that resolving my feelings about having children is
something I've always been dealing with, and have needed to
learn, and now finally have needed to give up and to begin to
see what is beneath the process.

I had spent a lot of time being obsessed with the thought of
children. Possession, I know, was part of it. I was never patient,
never waiting until a child came to me. I was always trying very
hard, hoping, desiring—not really accepting or seeing or
waiting, having faith. There is a difference between being
ready and open for gifts when they come, seeing them for what
they are, and forcefully trying to manipulate my environment.

I had a dream and hope of having babies back before Dick
and I were married, though I never thought of that as the
primary reason for marriage. I felt I wanted to always be with
him, and to somehow "belong" to him. But the idea of children
was somehow an expected part of it all.

Some years later when we were married, I had trouble
conceiving. There was the first baby I miscarried, then the
wonderful event of Richard's birth, then Marisa, then Johanna,
and finally the last miscarriage.

All those children passed through me in some way.

So now in my life, there is Richard, and in a small peripheral way there are Caitlin and Betsy, my little nieces.

Today I wonder why I was so intent on possessing children, and why the emphasis is always on perfect children instead of just hoping for a child who will teach us about life and love. Certainly the birth of Richard was incredible and I wouldn't have missed it, or the years since then, for all the world. It was reason enough to have been born myself. And the sad/sweet fleeting butterfly joy of Johanna is a treasure I hold dear.

At the same time I see with my heart so many more children now—children for whom my vision was clouded. I thought I could only love and really be touched by my children, but now I think even my concept of *my* is changed. The world is full of children who need so much. There is no scarcity. The only scarcity is how much I, or anyone else, want to give to them.

For a while I found myself befriending a child in my neighborhood, thin and with an undernourished look about her. I don't know if it is lack of food, or health, or love. But she came and sat on my doorstep, and other doorsteps on our block. I gave her an old necklace, pads of drawing paper, and crayons. I asked her to draw me a flower, and she told me she only draws guns. I always took a flower if she drew one, and told her I didn't really like guns. I tried to give her conversations and a little caring. And yet in all honesty, I realized after a while, my giving was limited. Perhaps if I had met her on her level, spent time looking at the guns in order to lead her to the flowers—but I've had to ask myself, How much am I really willing to give?

Within the first year after Dick died I volunteered for a few months at Children's Hospital in the playroom. I needed to feel involved with children, with people, with life. Too, I somehow wanted to feel I could touch the heart of life. I also wanted to be able to be around people/children who had physical problems, and to learn to see beyond that—to not be stopped from relating. So many times we don't see the person for the problem. I knew this was a lesson I needed. Last, but not least, people who write tend to sit back and observe life too much. I was now spending more time alone than I ever had, and I felt I needed some kind of meaningful human interchange.

192

There is a special intimacy you can feel when you've stopped the world and gone into the fantasy of a child's special magical world. I loved the moments there in the playroom when I felt connection with a child—when I sensed we had truly touched.

And I learned a great deal. One day a little girl, three or four, feeling fearful and alone, sat at the crafts table, uninterestedly holding a crayon in her hand. A little boy, perhaps five, stood next to her, dropping marbles down a slotted trail. They zigzagged back and forth until they plunked free at the bottom. Each time he set the marble out on its journey, he gleefully squealed and clapped his hands. His face was completely immersed in joy. I've never seen a child so happy. The happiness outshone the fact that the little boy was mongoloid, or Down's syndrome. I watched him, hesitantly at first. I had never been around many Down's syndrome children. After all, Johanna had been here only six months. This little boy's joy began to enrapture me, and I found it easy to truly drink him in for that little while. Then the little girl sitting next to him suddenly started weeping. She just sat there and tears came running down, and she began to sob. The boy held the next marble, ready to place it on the slot, and at the sound of her crying he stopped, suddenly, marble poised in midair, and he turned to her. He just stood there transfixed for half a minute, then with a rush of gusto he threw both his arms around her, hugged, and patted her.

I think it was one of the most wonderful moments of my life. Never had I seen anyone so completely involved in his or her moment—never so totally enjoying of an event, but so open to something else that took precedence, and so willing to give love the only way he knew how.

If there was a reason for my coming to the playroom, that had to be one of them.

But there were others. I began to notice a girl, thirteen years old. She was pretty and bright, and she was paralyzed from the waist down, with only minimal movement in her arms. I thought of Richard, the same age, and all I can say is I felt drawn to her. But I didn't do anything about it, didn't know what to do about it, until one day it occurred to me there was one thing she might be able to do—write poetry. She could type with a special attachment on her hand and I had seen her do this. I knew she would be very sensitive, perceptive, and aware, that her senses were probably all heightened, and that if she could be in touch with those feelings, or awakened to that fact, it might open doors. So I brought a copy of a poetry book I had written years ago with friends—simple thoughts and poems about nature and about feelings, and I left it for her with a note, hoping it would inspire or nudge her to write.

I missed seeing her, for as it turned out she was discharged within a few days, but I was glad I had reached out to her, however inadequate and shy my attempt. I felt in some ways she was a spiritual child of mine, that I had perhaps been drawn to her just to give her that part of myself. I hope it was enough, or that it was something at least that spoke to her.

A few weeks later I wrote a story for the *Tribune,* our San Diego evening paper. The subject was the adoption of Mexican babies. It involved my going to Tijuana with a photographer and visiting two orphanages. They say writing a good story changes you, and this was such a story. I came away with the feel of those children's hands in mine, and the light weight of their little bodies on my knees still with me. Their dark-eyed laughter rising like bright flowers from the dirt they played in hung in my ears and heart. It was overwhelming to know so many children have so little and that those children in the orphanages are in fact the lucky ones. Hundreds of others roam the streets and dumps of border cities like Tijuana every day. These children too are, in a sense, my children, all our children. There's no lack. How much am I able to give?

Last summer when Richard and I went on our trip, and stopped in Taos, I found a gallery I loved. The artist's pastel sketches were all of Navajo women; most alone, strong and detached, some with children, the women enclosing the children with their bodies, with their love. One sketch caught me immediately. I wanted it. It was in tones of pink and beige. The mother was suckling her baby at her breast. They were held in a moment of oneness, their eyes locked into each other.

But I fought my desire, my intuition, if you will. I told myself "You can't have that picture. You don't have a baby anymore. Johanna died. Richard is almost a teenager. You lost

194

the last baby you and Dick expected. Now you've lost Dick. You should buy a picture of a woman alone. . . ."

I picked up one of the pictures of a "strong alone woman," and walked to the desk to pay for it. Then I walked back, set it down. I didn't want any of those women. I wanted the picture of the mother and child. Then I suddenly realized—that picture was more than a mother and child—that picture was life nourishing life. I was still engaged in that—still a part of that. In fact the picture reinforced the feeling in me. It was the desire to hold and to be held, it was the I-Thou, the sense of communication, it was God and man, mother and of-mother, the desire to give and to receive. It was the little child in each of us, and that included Dick, and it was the procreator and nourisher in all of us too.

And it is also the particular, it is also a mother and a child, and I still have that relationship all my life on some level with Richard. It says somehow "I release my old desires," and at the same time, realize they always were fulfilled.

It was and is my picture.

What about the little child in Dick? The little child in each of us? If the basic nurturing experience which is part of us through our parents is somehow integrated so that we learn to nurture ourselves and others, then somehow the little child in Dick must have been lost—too wounded to think it deserved to live.

Maybe it is to recreate our initial experiences that we strive to progress once again through all of life's stages through our children. If the basic unblemished part of Dick was too innocent to protect itself and strive to live, then he may have identified with the innocent lives who came through me and ended so soon, and so in a sense their failures to live mirrored and forecasted his own failure to live.

Perhaps the child in Dick sought once again the void where he began, even before the parental womb-sea he once lived in. In his last years he had in fact gone back to the sea, from where we all have evolved. Through diving perhaps he re-experienced that primordial existence, and now he has completed the cycle and gone back one more step—to the nothingness—to the *all* where we truly begin and belong and even in life are connected.

# 20 / Shelter

Sometimes I've thought it is absolutely crazy that outwardly so many things seem the same. I'll be at the grocery store, and think, "My God—how can this be? After all that has happened—here I am, still shopping at Fed Mart." And there *is* outwardly a sameness. I live in the same house, have the same child, basically the same work. In a way it is as if he is just very very late for dinner. But of course he is never coming home. And so I am shedding who I was with Dick and gradually becoming who I am on another level. My work and life are growing, expanding, taking direction. And I don't feel the same inside.

Our house is probably the clearest symbol of the whole process, because though it is the same, it is becoming new also. A few rooms are repainted, I have new bookcases, some new pictures, and now the backyard is transformed. The old aluminum patio cover is torn down and a wooden deck built. Flowers are planted. It is a new area to live in—to be in.

So, as in the rest of my life, and Richard's too, we don't have

196

a new life. We have an extension of our old life, or of our lives as they continue.

There was a point, though, when I almost threw it all over, moved away, and toward the fantasy of a "new" life. But I came to my senses. To stay was a good choice for me, though I know it might not be for everyone.

We'd lived in our house for ten years. Richard was only three and one-half when we moved in. This was Johanna's home for her six months. The Christmas tree we bought the year she was born is planted in the backyard. Now it can be seen over the top of the house. This house has held friends and laughter. Memories are so thick I can almost smell them in the air.

We had made love and slept in the bedroom for nine years. We had eaten and shared conversations at the dinner table all those years. Fires in the fireplace had warmed our evenings, rain had fallen on the windowpanes, creating a haven inside. Dreams, hopes, and everyday life had lived here, were shared here. I remembered the year it took Dick to meticulously tile the bathroom, the pleasure he felt in the wood strips and wall coverings he had put up in the living room, the way he had painted RICHARD in large letters on our son's door, and I thought of the small room which had been an extra room, then Marisa's room, then Johanna's room, and finally my writing room.

After Dick's death I worked through the house slowly, began to put his belongings away a few at a time. First I cleared off the top of his dresser, then emptied his dresser drawers. Later I removed clothes from our closet. Later still I removed his jackets from the hall closet, putting most in boxes in the garage to be decided upon later. It is hard to deal with the leftovers of a person's life.

Security in those early months became important, and yet this was when the house was broken into for the first time—after a friend put in the dead bolts and peep hole. I had sought security and thought if certain precautions were maintained we were OK. My doors were locked, and so was my heart. I was still under the illusion we can protect ourselves. Could I secure the house? or Dick? Richard? myself?

197

All drawers were opened—letters and clothing spilled out onto the floor. I quickly checked for the one "treasure" I knew I had—a large diamond ring my father had left me twelve years ago when he died. The blue box was open, and empty. I had kept it all those years, never giving it a thought. Now that I wanted it, had even planned to take it the very next day to a jeweler to be remounted, it was gone. Amazing, I thought. Six months later I bought a tiny diamond with the five hundred dollars the insurance company had awarded me, and by then I realized a diamond means little to me. With this thought in mind I opened the drawer to place the tiny diamond in the ring box, and when I opened the box, the ring was there! I was stunned. As I looked through the drawer I realized there were two boxes very much alike. I had merely panicked and jumped to the conclusion it was stolen. What I found interesting about this is that when I no longer cared about a diamond, I suddenly had one, whereas before, just as I clung to the thought of it, it seemed to disappear.

As summer arrived, the urge to move away grew in me. I wanted to leave and begin a new life, as if that new life would magically happen in new surroundings. The idea appealed to me, and at the time this illusion seemed like a solution.

The process of grief applies to the house, too, because in the house are so many memories and so much life as we had lived it.

At first the house represented and was full of great sorrow and sadness. It was a heavy place. I half expected to see Dick reflected in the living room mirror he liked so much. When the antique light he'd restored burned out, I replaced the bulbs for him, not for me. Everything was empty and gray—was not our house anymore.

It was an empty dark shell to me. It felt blue, gray, and cold. Only the fires in the fireplace at night made the living room bearable, tolerable. I spent most evenings in my bedroom, even taking the TV back there, along with books to read. Only that room seemed truly mine. I felt imprisoned.

There was guilt too, I know, mixed in it all. If Dick's work drove him to his death, then this house was also a participant—

this place he had bought for us, and had worked to pay for.

Perhaps it was my anger that did not want to stay in the house, that wanted to desert it, the way I felt I had been deserted. I wanted to be free of memories, to escape to a clean, sterile, safe place.

I had a happy feeling about the thought of a move at first, even a sense of direction and purpose. We'd make a clean break, I decided—have new neighbors, new stores and a new school for Richard.

I'd seen some townhouses I liked. The image of them stayed in my mind, and nothing else looked quite so good. When I later took Richard there, he, too, was attracted to them. It began to feel good. At least it gave us a happy hope. I guess it was something to plan for and dream about. For that purpose it was sufficient.

When I put our house up for sale I tried to do it without emotion. I told myself I'd be glad to leave the dried paint on the garage floor, the backyard with its overgrown grass and ice plant, and even some of the neighbors. I rationalized that such an event as Dick's suicide called for a major change, that it somehow was even my duty.

In order to sell the house, I knew I needed to paint the back of the garage, to really scrub the cabinets, and to plant a few flowers.

Something began to happen to me gradually then.

As I painted one day on the back of the garage I began to realize I was "caring" for the house—for the first time. Dick had cared for it, but I hadn't—not ever. I only lived here, used it, but didn't really make contact with this—my shelter. I realized how full, how rich, this house has been.

One afternoon I went back over to the townhouse tract. The dwellings looked so sterile as I drove up to them—a stucco honeycomb.

I tried to push those thoughts down, but the seed was planted. I tried to feel as happy about them as I had before, but the thrill was gone.

I began to worry about my decision. At night I often lay awake until two or three in the morning. Anxiety sent chills up and down my body. I began to feel trapped in the situation.

199

Could I just turn around and take my house off the market?

I told myself I was a coward—that this was like pre-wedding anxiety, and I tried not to give in to it. But the feeling persisted.

I realized that emotionally it would be difficult to leave my house. This *did* feel like home. The feeling of security, in the sense of belonging, seemed right. Financially, it couldn't be beat. Somehow my mind had glossed over all the figures. Now they began to march through my brain like so many Nazi soldiers.

Suddenly the decision became clear to me. The fantasy existence I had imagined in the new place shifted in my mind. I knew we belonged here for now. My mind had started to move back into the house. Now I wanted to take it over.

This was our home, where my memories once lived as real events. This was my house where new events could also be born. Some things could stay—others would go. I could make changes—turn it into my house and Richard's house.

Richard had also come full circle. He didn't want to leave his friends, his school and teachers. His loss was not so searing if we stayed here.

I began to truly question *why* we always want to escape from our past. We can't anyway. We only take it with us. The pain of loss, the questions would go on until they had finished their work on me. And there would be no new life waiting for us in that house. I'd have to make my new life—my career, my social life. These were still partial spaces, not completely filled in.

One thing was settled now at least. I'd chosen to live in the house. Now it wasn't so much that we were left here, but now we had come back to it with strength and choice.

I painted the fireplace "inside-of-sea-shell pink." The rosy-beige tone also reminded me of the pink mesas we had seen on our trip through New Mexico. The print of the huge white shell fit well there. I set a starfish and an abalone shell on the hearth. I liked it. This was not sad and empty, but struck me as being true to my life. Little by little the house became mine—gradually, the way a shell thrown up on the beach changes ever so slightly as the light of the day changes, with new shadows, new spots of light. The shells seemed to symbolize my house, my life, for now. Seashells are empty, but beautiful. They've had life, and they'll have it again, perhaps, in another form. Hermit sea creatures can come to stay in a shell for a while. And I like the sturdiness and symmetry of the shells.

I began to not be afraid of the house, as I had been for a while. I began to embrace it and appreciate the wounds it carried. They were, after all, mine.

I'd never thought of a house having a soul, though I'd heard the notion, but I could feel it in the house now—all the laughing, all the loving, and the tears too. And I began to see it as an unfinished art work—something to play around with, and express myself with.

Before I had expressed myself *inside* the house. It was only the covering, the shelter. Now the shelter itself could be expression as I chose ways to decorate it so that it reflected me.

The day they took the "For Sale" sign down in front, I had emotionally bought it. This was our home now. Richard's and mine. This was our new life, opening more every day. I couldn't really throw away and desert what we had. I didn't need to. We had lived here as a family, and we had lived here as individuals too. Because Dick had gone away didn't necessarily mean I had to go away too. I could work and grow from here.

> Now the house
> begins to be full
> of my son and me.
>
> You're more gone now
> than even a few months ago.
> Your presence doesn't fill
>    all the spaces anymore.
>
> It is warm. Air moves.
> I live here.
>
> Plants thrive.
> The dog walks, then sleeps.
> The door bangs with a boy's going out.

That's life now—
learning to grow away from each other.

(September 17, 1979)

Now—as I sit on the new deck I had built in back, in the sunshine, with flowers around, most I've planted—pink bushes of hawthorn bristle, and dark brilliant fuchsia pansies gently bow and move. Birds flutter and chirp in the birdbath. This new space I've made feels like a beginning platform.

Journal entry, March, 1980:
The sun, the flowers speak aliveness to me. Breeze moves across. Mozart on a tape recorder charms me. Birds chirp, unaware of me. I've sat here long enough today that they accept me.

It's time to spend spaces of time here—being and sensing—and a time to work now—perhaps a time to begin to love now.

And because there is a place to come to now—I can also go from it.

It feels a little like the first garden—where innocence reigned.

# 21 / First Anniversary

It's funny the way we give power to dates, or places, when the truth is the event no longer exists, and a day is simply another day. But our minds have constructed a connection; 365 days after a particular event will be significant in relation to that event. Of course the sun will be in the same place in the sky, but new gases explode on the now older sun—new clouds move listlessly across the sky. Still our minds remember.

The date of Dick's death, one year later, stopped the flow of the beginning unfolding life I felt in me. I was afraid of that date, afraid I would relive the horror of that night. I felt it was essential to a healthy state of mind to not be in my house during that night, to not feel the living room take on the colors of pain.

So Richard and I planned a train trip to Santa Barbara. We'd been there before, several times in the past, and it felt like a positive place to be.

We left on November 2, the first anniversary of the night Dick hadn't come home, and we spent one night. The next day, November 3, the date of his actual death, we rode the

203

train home. The next day I recorded our trip in my journal. I felt somehow I was a step freer by making it through those two days.

Journal entry, November, 4, 1979:
Over the hump. It's over a year now—a year yesterday.

We took the train to Santa Barbara. In my mind, though I tried not to, I found myself retracing the steps—a little like the steps of the cross I guess.

We left on the 7:00 A.M. train. As we came close to Santa Barbara, it was approaching noontime and I remembered that on this day last year I was working at my job at UCSD—that I was probably making plans to meet Dick for lunch. As the train pulled in it was almost 1:00 P.M., almost time for our last encounter.

At the motel as I made a phone call at a pay phone and watched a man swim in the pool, I remembered at that time we probably were sharing the salad we had for lunch together.

When Richard and I took the bus to downtown Santa Barbara I knew it was at this time that we last touched and kissed, that he walked away and only stood and looked at me—that as this bus full of pleasant people in this pleasant, sunny city of Santa Barbara sped toward the center of town, a year ago, Dick was looking at me for the last time, looking at me without being able to say goodbye. Then he had turned and walked away.

Later in, of all places, McDonald's, I noticed it was 4:00 P.M., and I remembered at this time I had called Dick to tell him I had won a ten-dollar prize in a recipe contest. It was just a funny, happy communication. He said, "That's neat, Karen." And then he seemed to be busy. I don't remember exactly what he said, but I had heard his voice for the last time.

That is one thing that can haunt—to never hear some- one's voice again. We try to imagine—to remember that particular intonation, that particular timbre, but it is lost—harder even than remembering colors.

Later in a bookstore, I noticed the time—knew by now I had expected him home, by now was worried. As we walked among D. H. Lawrence, C. S. Lewis, Ursula LeGuin, I tried not to think of the choking panic I had begun to feel one year ago.

For dinner Richard and I went to a wonderful Greek restaurant, La Plaka, where we had all gone a few years ago. I noticed as we were there, that the night was coming on more intensely, and in that time I felt myself pull back from memories. I didn't want to remember or think of it anymore. It was too much.

I had a wonderful time with Richard, eating our Greek food. I looked at him and realized how totally I love him. Not that there's no love left for anyone else, but that I love him completely. He is Dick's and my beautiful child—and he has perhaps the best of both of us. He is also and more importantly a person I like—for himself.

So, having a happy talk with Richard as he told me how nice his girlfriend is, as we laughed about Mork from Ork—as he ordered shish kebab and baklava and noticed that they played the same record over and over again (though to most people all Greek music sounds alike). This was after all the best way to spend this anniversary.

We took a taxi back to the motel and Richard soon fell asleep. I read and thought that I should say a prayer for Dick—at least be mindful of him, and yet the thoughts on this evening were too painful. I fell asleep, perhaps wanting to blot out the day. It felt like a river I needed to swim to the other side of. I felt safe in Santa Barbara—felt it would have been dangerous, frightening, to be in San

Diego. I guess I fell asleep feeling I had escaped, that I had found a temporary refuge.

I awakened. It seemed hours and hours later. I felt alert, untired, thought I might get up early to take my shower, or I might read for a while. I lay and thought for a few minutes. Then I decided to turn on the light. It must be 5:00 A.M. or so, I thought. But with the light on I saw it was only past 11:30 P.M. The night was in no way over. In fact it had just begun. I had a strange tension that night. It's funny how just knowing the date can do that.

I got up and took one Valium, the last one I had—and I'd had this one for months—but this felt like an emergency. I knew or feared that without it I would not be able to relax and let go into healing sleep, and I couldn't bear to lie awake and think too much that night.

With the help of the sedative, or my body deciding it would sedate itself, I did sleep. When it was morning I got up, showered, and we went for breakfast. I didn't say anything to Richard about the anniversary, though he may have been aware of it and thought of it, but I didn't want to cause guilt or heaviness, and I didn't want this new day ruined, or the shadow of that day a year ago to weigh on his young shoulders. Why should it? It really was just another day. Only my mind had colored it. And still, it is important to remember the joy and the good times, but that can be done any day.

So I tried to let the new day flow like a golden river. We went to the zoo. We looked in the shops. It rained and we hopped across puddles. We were alive that day. That's all. That's everything.

I wrote this poem on the train coming home to San Diego, later that day, as we moved along parallel to the evening sea. In a sense it is another way of saying goodbye. It had been a year.

206

They say a person is pretty much over grief in a year, but goodbye, like love, can't be measured.

*For Dick*
The ocean is wearing its blue lace dress
The train whistles in the distance,
meaning nothing.
We move on.

I wanted to touch your hand today,
but it slipped past me
like a shell I tried to hold
already
tumbling
back
into the sea.

(November 3, 1979)

# 22 / Work

To dip our hands in the rawness of life, and come up with something glistening and gleaming—or to press the muck between our palms and find that we have made a star—are for me examples of work.

For work is cultivation—the joy of creation. To fill hours for a paycheck is not necessarily work, though it could be if a person happens to find his or her work there. Sometimes I think work is just understanding someone who happens to inhabit the workspace next to you, or of course it could be something really phenomenal like discovering the DNA helix. There's a wide range, but none of it makes any sense without love and struggle.

Finding my work, it seems to me, is one of the most important facets of growth and finding my own life since Dick died. I don't think I truly knew the meaning of the word before. I had felt the power of writing in me. I wrote articles when something interested or affected me, and each time I was dipping into the barrel and tasting this joy of work, but I didn't know what it was like to be consumed, to be dedicated, to really use myself or feel steady purpose. The process was spotty and ephemeral, only occasionally touching ground.

Now I think if there is a question to be answered in our lives this seeking for purpose must be integral with it. I didn't, before, ever feel true purpose beyond expression, and something I called fulfillment, which vaguely meant to me that I should become all that I could be—that I would then be "me." Everything stopped with the self. That was the culmination. The truth is everything *begins* with the self.

My job at UCSD was my lifesaver. I think my work there was just to heal a little bit, and to learn the beginning of love, new love on the other side of my pain. I feel that in many ways my friends there taught me more about love than I had ever known before—that if I could have taken that love and given it to Dick, he wouldn't have died, couldn't have died. Ironically though, of course, without the loss, I wouldn't have really seen those people or their love. It was a high price to pay.

I think, too, it was essential for me to be there in the university environment and experience the balancing of my anger for the university system with the good people I personally knew there. They were all very much a part of the drama, almost like a Greek chorus—defining, repeating, being there.

When I had visited the place where Dick died, that visit essentially cut the cord for me there. I was convinced then I didn't want to work on campus anymore. It was just time to go. I could no longer bear to be part of it. My painful feelings for the university and for Dick surfaced. There were good people, and many had gone through their own pain and transformation because of his death, but too many stories were going around—how the students felt who saw him fall, why he did it. I don't really know most of the stories, and I guess I really don't want to. I felt then that if I wanted to live, I had to leave my job and that campus—go no deeper into Dick's death from that standpoint. From then on, I told myself, I wanted every step I took to be a step up, a step toward more life and more light.

After quitting that job I started freelancing and also continued with teaching. With my work I began to gradually see

209

purpose and direction. I had written poems all my life, and articles for eight years or so. But now that writing became more and more not only my expression, but my full-time work; more than that, my way to deal in the world, my way to learn and pass it on, and learn again—a one-way dialogue with a world of people I would not probably meet. Interviews with various people were always interesting, and I liked the connection there—the trust and understanding, the openness that often happened. These kinds of talks were limited, and the sharing was usually one time, but there is a different kind of satisfaction in that too. And both the interviewer and the person interviewed are involved in bringing to light something that one hopes reaches, touches others.

The classes in writing I had begun to teach fulfilled in me even more my need for purpose. I felt it was important I help others break the silence Dick couldn't break. I knew expression had always helped me, and so I felt part of my purpose had to be to help others feel safe and encouraged about their expression. In the beginning, too, I probably went overboard in my dedication to this idea, but I know it gave me something to point toward. And of course the truth is my students have always given me every bit as much as I have ever given them.

Journal entry, May 8, 1980:
A woman in my class last night told me that after her father died things were very hard for her mother, and that at one point her mother held her and her brother in her arms, and jumped.

This woman now has been widowed herself, though now she is remarried. She carries the scars of those losses, and I can see she has triumphed.

I wonder about all these connections.
I wonder too that my writing class has become so much a forum of people's feelings and opinions. Maybe it is because I feel so much that is what is important. The people who only want surface structure drop out—the ones who want to touch their hearts—and share—stay.

Everything is really as it should be.

Since Dick couldn't express himself, at least not verbally, not enough directly, then I began to feel a strange balance every time a student wrote something from his or her heart, every time someone touched his or her soul, pain, observation, anger, or love—each time that happened I felt a bird had been set free, something had escaped that had been caged. I can't listen now to Dick's words or nurture their delivery, but I can observe that sometimes in others. We are all crying out in some way. We need each other.

Recently I ran a workshop at a drug rehabilitation center. I felt a little fearful that I wouldn't be able to reach the people there, that I wouldn't speak their language, that they wouldn't accept me, that I wasn't dominant enough to work with them. What I discovered is that they were just human beings trying to get their lives together, people in transition who've gone through some hard things, that it isn't easy, and that they are struggling—and making it. And I discovered they were truly gifted. None of them had written much before. One man had written some poems, but most had only written letters, and even that seldom. Yet without fail, each participated in the exercise, and each wrote a poem! This is rare. In writing classes the majority of people will balk at poetry—say they can't write it, and won't. At least that has been my experience. At the rehabilitation house, they said they couldn't, but then they did.

One man who had spent time in solitary confinement while in prison wrote a poem about seeing a sunset behind prison bars. Another, an addict for twenty-one years, wrote a love poem, spoke of wanting to see tenderness in another's eyes—another young man wrote of Vietnam, of the awful colors of the sky laced with death.

When I left that day, I felt—this is work, this has purpose. It seemed to go beyond a little bit, and yet it gave to me. And true work I think maybe has that ability inherent in it, to *give* to the worker, and to teach the worker.

Maybe the purpose we find is an extension past ourselves, an overflow toward some goal, some "other"—a grappling with the mysteries—and it is the need to understand, no matter how limited that understanding may seem.

211

So I feel my basic work must be to break the silence, to speak the words no one wanted to speak before, or couldn't, and maybe to also help others break their silence, and then to learn to reshape the energy into a form that adds to the world, that gives some form, or order, or beauty.

As I write this book, it is my work, my creation I am shaping from Dick's and my past, my present, Richard's present, and my mind. It has a purpose and a life of its own.

I think Dick did not have the time to find his true work. He was too busy making a living. True work would have nurtured him. But the "job" destroyed him.

I feel that in some ways a lot of what we are all searching for is the work of learning finally to see, really see others, ourselves. Our work is to live, grow, learn—to begin to start trying to love. Maybe love isn't just always a gift that is handed to us. Maybe sometimes we have to make it, create it for ourselves, and acknowledge it in others, and we might have to work at that.

# LIGHT

Leave
spaces
where daisies need to grow

Leave
places
where you might want to go,

Don't rush in,
fill it up,
or step on
what is there.

Leave spaces,
and places,
for traces
of beginnings
to go.

# 23 / Alone—All One

Journal entry: January 1980:
Every joy, every sadness, we do go through basically
alone—and so where does it begin—the aloneness? It
always is, and will be—as is—as it should be. I began to see
it always was my feelings, my experience, my feeling of
love, my resolution of anger or hurt—and then it was, at
last—to look in someone's eyes, and know they know this
too.

When I think back I realize loneliness did not start when
Dick died. It was always a part of me during our marriage,
except for brief moments. But it did not start then either. It
was a part of me before. The illusion was that marriage would
bring an end to the feeling of separation. Later I thought
having babies would end the feeling, bring a sense of wholeness. It is true—there have been moments, but there was, and
is, an undercurrent in me that always seeks. And I guess it is in
all of us.

Dick's death caused me to finally have to come face to face

215

with that feeling, and so, in some ways, I feel less lonely now. Perhaps running away is what causes the loneliness, while being in touch brings a sense of aloneness.

The illusion that there was someone to share my life, my dreams, my joys, and my sadnesses, my bed, and my meals was broken suddenly like a soap bubble. I had always thought whatever happened in life, Dick and I would go through it together. I had never allowed myself to think of the ending.

A deep feeling of loneliness was not the first feeling after his death, but it was a fact that I was alone. Horror, terror, disbelief, unfulfilled yearnings—these I felt first. I think there was not enough of a relationship with myself or the world during that first year to even experience or be in contact with my own sense of isolation.

In the early weeks, I reacted to the fact of dreadful insecurity by sleeping on my son's bottom bunk. I did this for six weeks, until our Christmas trip. I couldn't bear to go into the bedroom except to get changes of clothing. The bedroom just represented too much. I couldn't sleep in the living room on the couch, because all I could think of there was the nightmare of that night—the way I had sat on that couch and waited. And I guess, too, I needed creature closeness. Richard always went to bed first, climbing onto his top bunk. The dog slept in there too—on the floor on his special blanket. I came in a little later, lay down on the bottom bunk and huddled under the blankets like a shipwreck victim.

Occasionally I would take a Valium to just take the edge off my anxiety and relax me. Sometimes I awakened several times during the night, but usually I would sink back into sleep. In fact I looked forward to the night and to sleep. The important thing to me for a while seemed to be just getting through the day, so that I could go to sleep again and try to blot it all out. Each night I fell asleep and dreamed of Dick—always the same dream, though slightly different visually. In each dream I was feeling great love for him, and trying to tell him this. I had my arms around him, but he never sensed or heard me. Each time I awakened and remembered he was gone. Then the feeling it was too late to ever tell him or show him I loved him anymore would sweep over me. This, I think, is one of the hardest

216

things about any kind of sudden death—to feel suddenly cut off and left to try to fit the pieces of the relationship together alone. Maybe this is especially true with suicide. For a long time I felt Dick was psychically cut off from me. This brought feelings of loneliness.

Gradually, the dreams ended. One of the later ones I recorded in my journal.

Journal entry, January, 1979:
*Dream:* I was in a pillow-covered room with Dick. We were both lying down. I realized he was barely alive. I tried to breathe life into him, but after a while I realized I couldn't—that it was too late. And so I moved over to the other side of the room.

After Richard and I returned from the Christmas trip I moved into the bedroom that had been Dick's and mine. Now it was mine alone. I repainted the room a sunny, buttery yellow. I put a different covering on the bed—a quilt someone had given me. I bought a new picture to hang on the wall (a poster—serigraph—of Emily Dickinson) and moved the bed to the far side of the room. Now I could bear to be in there by myself. It was the beginning of "my" room. I still slept only on my side of the bed, though, and I always kept the hall light on, and the door cracked open. This continued until almost a year later.

Then one day I bought some sheets and a bedspread that looked like a soft watercolor rainbow. I came home, moved my bed to the opposite side of the room, rearranged the dressers, and from that night on I sleep in the middle, or wherever I want to, and I close the door and I turn off the light.

At first loneliness was tied up with all the things I associated with Dick. No one would ever drive up in that 1970 Datsun station wagon with the dent on the side again at 5:30 every evening. He wouldn't be there to call during the day. When the phone rang, it would never be his voice. He would never be there to kiss and love me—to talk to me. Certain songs reminded me of him—the Eagles—Janis Joplin. I would never

217

be able to fix something I thought he would like for dinner, or make him a batik T-shirt. From now on all my articles would be finished and turned in without reading and sharing them with him, without his opinion. I hadn't realized how much I'd relied on his opinion. Now, all choices were mine.

Dick, Richard, and I would never all three sit down to meals again, never go to Los Angeles to the Art Museum and the Tar Pits together, and never again have what Richard used to call "an all-family hug." But the worst loneliness was not that there was no one in bed next to me, but that I felt no one would ever know me the way Dick knew me. I had invested thoughts and feelings for nineteen years—all the important and unimportant events of my life were shared with Dick. And with few exceptions he had known everyone I had ever loved, everyone who had been important in my life. He had known my mother, and had met my father. He had known my grandmother. He and I had experienced the life of Johanna together. I felt that the one person who knew my life had taken all of that and left. I felt separated not only from Dick, but from parts of myself. When he was gone, it seemed that almost everything was gone, and that the people I'd loved and lost before had now been lost again.

In a way I felt Dick had killed a lot of me when he died. Our plans for the future were interwoven. I had always imagined "our future," not "my future." Hopes and plans—for Richard, for other children we might have, for work—were our common dreams, as were our memories, a blend of each other's.

I think it is true that a lot of me, of my past, did die at that point, but what remains is mine, and what is growing is mine. He just took his reflection of those people that belonged to him, and he ended his dreams and his future, but not mine and not Richard's. He took only himself—that gift which was never mine, never Richard's even, only shared with us for a while.

When I went out to be with people I was very aware that many knew what had happened to Dick, and so at first it was difficult going anywhere. I always saw people we had known. It was even harder to see the people who didn't know what had happened and realize I would then have to go through it all again, would have to tell them. Then they would inevitably say, "Do you have any idea why he did it?" I would try to say all I knew, and then my throat would begin to ache and get tight, and I knew I just couldn't keep talking about it.

I began to have the feeling when I was with people that I didn't belong to anyone anymore. It was a new feeling, hard to adjust to. I would find myself bringing Dick into the conversation, just in a casual sense—"My husband liked this—or that." It made me still feel connected. But I wasn't connected. I was cut off, and I was also cut off from myself. I was hanging on to threads. It took a long time to not bring Dick with me, in a sense, wherever I went, and to gain a new awareness of myself.

Journal entry, February, 1980:
I think that the reality of what happened began to truly sink in after the first year.

It's not true you are over it by then. How impossible. There is no such thing, I think, as getting over it. It is a new reality I have to learn to live in.

I began to wear thin a year and a few months afterwards. Sort of as if my steam had all gone. I was tired of being the perfect suicide survivor.

I had been brave. I had even written my essay for *Newsweek,* appeared on TV shows. I had managed the money, I had quit crying after a few months, I had taken good care of Richard, made good decisions about buying a car, and about not moving. I was moving ahead in my writing. I did everything just right. I was "a good girl." Nothing was out of place.

But I just began to crumble, and to be irritable.

I think I was just truly feeling my loneliness. I had been holding everything up so well, and still no one was there to hold me up.

219

It was as if I had to finally give birth to his death, and to let it go on its way, as a separate entity, before I could really become my own aloneness. Before that, I was pregnant with his death.

As I began to release more of what I was holding onto—guilt, grief—I could finally be more alone in the best sense, alone with myself, in solitude, not lonely and left.

Gradually the loneliness began to change to aloneness, and with that aloneness came somewhat a sense of all-oneness, that we are all connected. I began to feel from deep inside that we all have hopes, fears, we all need love, and we all have the potential to give love. The separateness is the illusion.

I didn't think the direction for me was to just believe some one person would come to fill the void. I felt the answer was deeper and had to do with facing that void and realizing what I have and who I am.

Somewhere along the way I started to look inside myself. I came to the point where I didn't coddle myself like a baby, or think of myself as someone who has faced tragedy. I started to feel really lucky to be living my life—and I started to go into that aloneness instead of running away from it. Until then—perhaps a year later—I had fought it. I had wanted people, noise, busyness. But gradually I began to want quiet, to feel peace. I wanted to gaze on a candle flame or a white rose. I began to like and need to have times alone, and to center myself and touch base. I began to feel that I was finally empty, in a good sense—clean—and now I could put in what I wanted, what felt right. The emptiness did not feel lacking—there was a fullness to it. It seems to me our creativity and love and sense of oneness are deep inside in that quiet place. I didn't want just comfort or distraction anymore, or to merely fill up my days. I wanted to touch the heart of life.

It seems to me now the transition between alone and all one is never really completed. It is something to be aware of and to be open to.

Going into myself was necessary in order to begin to go out of myself. The result of being by myself (that is without a mate, because I do have Richard and I do have friends), is that I have become more particular and careful about my time. Once I was

220

no longer afraid to be alone I could then put into my life what was important to me. This has to do with people, and it has to do with how I spend work time. I no longer need to be with people just for the sake of not being alone, but I now want to be with certain people because they are special to me.

The quality of a few hours spent with a very special friend means much more to me than several evenings and phone calls from someone who means less. Loneliness is perhaps being out of touch with ourselves, but also out of touch with someone who matters. Quantity of time and closeness isn't essential.

To have someone I truly love just touch the tips of my fingers or share a dream or thought with me can give such joy. Quantity is not a measure of love. Since I haven't felt the need to fill up my loneliness, my needs have been less, and I have felt exquisitely sensitive to beauty in its fineness more than in its abundance. A glimpse of a rainbow, even if you never see one again, is worth much more than a week of overcast days. I feel more prepared for magic and beauty. Maybe this is because shock and loss can set us free, and so can aloneness and solitude. Maybe we need to learn to live alone before we can really be with another.

I have realized, too, that in a way we always are alone. And for that very reason we are not alone, because we are together in that. I lived with Dick, but my dreams and hopes and hurts always seemed mine. Today my life-style remains much the same, so maybe it always was my life-style. I suppose we were living side by side, together in our aloneness. We were sharing our journeys—alone—together. The paradox of knowing we don't really know another, and yet we are one another.

To be alone is to be at one, is to be whole—but the wholeness doesn't come from outside, from others, from marriage, children. It comes from within to be shared with others. We are all whole, but often can't comprehend this until much is stripped away, and then we begin to see ourselves and others.

When I have written articles and people have responded, this has also caused me to feel that in many ways we all are truly one. It is not really an overly idealistic thought. The hundreds of people who wrote to me after the *Newsweek* article

221

showed me this, by their response, their sharing, their love.

Oneness is also as simple as knowing myself, loving myself. I think maybe that is why I believe it is necessary to rid ourselves of guilt and self-flagellation when someone close to us has committed suicide. It is easy to punish ourselves, but it is not only not good for us, it is not good for the world. Maybe when we destroy ourselves and the oneness inside, or parts of ourselves, we destroy part of the world, because we are all connected, and when we save ourselves, in our wholeness, we save others too.

And if we all are one, then those who choose to take their lives are also one with us, not something "other." We can't partition them off as if they are different. They are often people who just couldn't take the stresses of ordinary life. Some people are hardy, perhaps weedlike—survivors. Others are too sensitive—or too rigid. They perhaps cannot bend, and so, in their fragility, break. Some people can make it, and some people can't. They are all us. Some of us never come close to the act of suicide. Others do come close. We often don't want to acknowledge this connection because it is frightening, but it is more frightening to deny it, and harder on the survivors. And we are all survivors, too, in a sense.

We are all held in the balance between our life forces and our death wishes. We are all capable of everything. Primitive cultures have always recognized this. Maybe the notion of "possession" comes from this possession by the destructive forces or death wishes within us. We all potentially hold on to life, nurture life, and give life, and we all potentially can let go of, or take life. I picture it sometimes as a great wheel. Some people are close to the center—to themselves—and to God, or light, or creation. They are involved in life. Others, just by the sheer centrifugal force, are connected and interacting with each other. Others, near the edge, may be falling off, perhaps due to that same force. They are further from the hub of life. They are not as highly involved in this life. They, too, may be close to themselves, but on a different level almost. They are barely connected to the wheel, are separate, discrete, and are easily flung off, or perhaps they just let go.

222

No one will ever love me quite the way Dick did, and still I have that love inside. He cared about my past struggles and about my present strengths and joys, but he couldn't come into the future with me. And yet in my separation from him, there is coming a sense of completeness and wholeness and the sense of an evolving future.

One morning I was meditating, as I occasionally do, and I had a vision of friends, of people who were and are in my life—supportive of me—and I saw Richard. When I saw Richard I felt tears in my eyes, and I realized what a wonderful gift I have in him, and in my friends too. I just felt peace, and richness, very complete. And I felt or sensed the words, "You have never been alone, Karen," and I remembered that there has always been someone or someones—my mother, my brother, Dick, now others—and that it always seemed to be the right person or persons.

The next day, while talking to a doctor friend who had known us during the time we had Johanna, I mentioned the *Newsweek* article and the letters, and he said those very words to me. He said, "You have never been alone, Karen, have you?" And I haven't—and even if there comes a time in my life when I am truly all by myself, I think now there doesn't have to be the feeling of loneliness or separation, but all-oneness in the best sense of the word.

> The last woman on earth
> is beyond reach.
>
> She has outlived them all.
> She has reached a kind of lonely climax.
>
> The last woman on earth
> has a heart of crystal,
> reflecting only the sun.
>
> She remembers babies and birth,
> hearthfires and love.

The last woman on earth
has no more need for poems
   taped inside her wrists,
has no more need for tiny flowers
   pressed in her palms.

She steps outside herself,
lives where the air
   is scarce and precious.

                                   (January 5, 1980)

# 24 / Rebirth

There is perhaps no final goodbye, any more than there can ever be a hello that goes on forever, yet we can say goodbye more and more, and feel turning points, release, and learn to let go more and more.

I thought I had finished a great deal, but discovered more unraveling, more release, more birth, waiting for me. I discovered, too, that as with all the really important things in life, the only way we can really come to these points is alone.

Around a year after Dick's death, I realized how unfree I was in some ways. There was fear I hadn't faced, and I had attached it specifically to his place of death. I avoided the area, and couldn't even mention it without feeling anxiety.

For a long while I put it out of my mind, but one day, driving with a friend, we passed the area. I remember interrupting his conversation and saying, "I have to say this—I never drive past this area. It is where Dick died. It feels like a negative force field to me." He said, "But it is a beautiful area. You shouldn't have to feel that way." I knew this was so, but I didn't have the courage then to meet that challenge.

A few months later, as I began writing this book, I started to feel distress and fear even mentioning the place. During the same time I had a dream (this after a particularly happy day). It was the first dream of Dick I had had for months. Always before in my dreams I had felt a yearning for him and an unyielding, untouchable aspect to him. In this dream it seemed he now wanted to come back. I sensed this was no longer right. "Not now," I said in my dream, "that can't be anymore. It is too late." I had the feeling I needed to release him, and I began to feel strongly that what I needed to do was to return to the place of his death—that I had unfinished business there. I felt I might somehow be holding on to his spirit by not being able to say goodbye. During this time I even bought the Tibetan Book of the Dead, and read it. It seemed clear to me there was something I needed to come to terms with, make peace with, make friends with.

Still, I didn't know if I could face going to that place. The thought continued to nag at me, and I decided that maybe I might ask my friend to come with me, that since I loved our friendship, and it brought joy, that somehow bringing love and joy to a place of fear could be enough to overpower that fear.

I asked him what he thought of the idea. I had mixed feelings, and still I felt a strong need to ask. But he said to me, "No, I can't do that for you. You have to take that journey alone." It was a message of love. I had to heal myself of my fear, and save my own life at the spot where Dick had left his. My friend was right, but I couldn't see that right away. I felt alone. I felt rejected—even felt wrong that I had asked, felt I had gone too far, and ruined our friendship. All my feelings of loss seemed to well up in me. I was unable to see that I had to let go of the clinging, of fear, and that I needed to trust. All my fear seemed to come together in a point.

I didn't know how to cope with this sensation. I knew I needed to go to the area, but I just didn't know if I could. The next day I kept feeling anxiety, as if the place of his death were pulling on me. I felt an urge to go immediately to the spot, and still I felt that to go with those anxious feelings wasn't right somehow. My friend, Robin, happened to call, and asked me over for tea. Going to her house for tea was appropriate, and

226

calming. By doing that I delayed my immediate urge to go and just went with the day as it presented itself. Richard seemed to sense my turmoil. He hung around me during most of the day, as if he were aware of the urgency inside.

It was not yet time to face the fear, not when such a jumble of fear seemed to loom inside me. I needed to find some peace first and come to terms with going alone, and then I could come to terms with actually being there.

That night Richard had plans. He spent the night with a friend. I faced an evening alone. I decided to go out to a movie. Later I came home, read for a while, and fell asleep.

Though I don't remember my dreams, I think my mind worked some healing wonders on me, because when I awakened, I felt I understood. I realized it all had to do with letting go—fear of death produced clinging in me, and the inability to face that spot, that fear. I needed to be able to let go and to sense completion, to sense perfection, to let Dick go—in love. I felt I could do it that morning.

And something physical happened to me also. I began to bleed, though it wasn't my period.

It was a beautiful Sunday morning, and I felt complete. I felt peace and I knew I could and would go to UCSD alone.

That morning I had planned to go to a Zendo to learn more about meditation. The Zendo was in a beautiful rural area near Del Mar.

The sitting cleared my mind, and when I left I started on my trip to the campus. It was even on my way home.

I bought coffee—sat by the ocean for a few minutes, then started the car, drove up through Torrey Pines Park, and into the parking lot closest to the area.

I felt fearful as I drove into the parking lot. My hands became moist and my heartbeat grew stronger.

I parked and began to walk, thinking that though I was near I still had a distance to go. To my amazement I was very close. I walked through some arches, and suddenly saw it. I walked around a large space of grass and sat fifty or sixty feet away. Fear was still in me. I tried taking deep breaths and I looked at what was around me—the windows of the dormitory, filled

227

with students' paraphernalia, drawings, bottles, towels hanging out to dry. Music came from a distance. A few students walked around. I looked at them—these were not people who had been cruel or punishing to Dick. These were just students, trying to find their own way in life. I looked at the tops of the buildings, not just the one Dick had last stood on. They really were just tops of buildings. A building is just a building to house people, I thought. It has no special power of its own. And the breeze was soft, good. It gently blew the leaves—the delicate silver-dollar eucalyptus leaves.

A tightness was in my throat—a crying and hurting from deep inside, wanting to come out but not ready yet. I decided to get up and walk around. I walked past the spot. Sunlight flickered through leaves and on the cement. This was a path I needed to walk.

I went around another building and approached the area from another angle. I felt a need to physically make contact with the trees or grass. I ran my hand across some leaves, and I decided to sit in the grass. I touched the green blades. They were new. The grass growing when Dick left had been cut long ago.

I began to feel what I sensed as the presence of God, or goodness—this was not an evil place. This place was good. It felt clean. It felt not dark, but light. Something had happened here—a physical ending, a change took place. Other endings and transformations had taken place before. When Dick had made his decision to die—that was a death, and I don't know where that occurred. There is no way to pinpoint something like that. Did he die at the top—did his spirit leave then at the highest point? Did it really matter?

The air seemed effusive. The energy was not contained in a square of concrete like a black hole. There was a feeling of expansion here, not of constriction.

I sat in the grass and I said "The Lord's Prayer" to the grass and to the trees—and to the loving feeling I sensed. It seemed the right thing to do.

Then I knew I could leave. I could come again, or not, but the next time I came to UCSD I would not feel that old fear. I had made friends with it today. I had sat closer and closer to it.

228

It didn't have the power I had imagined, and no one could save me from it either. Only myself.

As I left I thought of how Dick had at times, many times, loved this campus, and he had walked all over it. He knew all parts of it.

We had shared a lot here—walks, concerts, talks, art shows. There was hurt here, but a lot of goodness was here too.

As I got into the car and drove away, I looked back, and tears came now. It was that point of joy and of pain too—and of release.

The day was exquisite and beautiful—tiny white flowers climbed the hillside, the sky was blue, all the greenery seemed to be almost singing in chorus.

I remembered the love and wonder I had felt here before. It was still here.

Dick didn't mean to take away the goodness. I had taken it away by my thought patterns, and I knew so surely that I couldn't have brought someone along today, thinking that person was my source of love and life, thinking he could exorcise the darkness here. That wouldn't have been fair to do to anyone, and that wouldn't have been right for me, or for Dick's memory. The journey was mine.

I had to come with love and life in me, and just see clearly.

By not coming with me, my friend had given me a gift of wings. My job was to come to release Dick and to release myself, and to set us both free in our separate paths now—in love.

I had come to that spot to say goodbye, and I had come to that spot to say hello.

> "Come to the edge."
> "We'll fall."
> "Come to the edge."
> "No, No, we're afraid we'll fall."
> "Come to the edge!"
> So they came
> and he pushed them
> and they flew.
> *(author unkown)*

229

Journal entry: March 31, 1980:
Dreamed I was going to walk all the way to Dick's office—
to the campus—a long way. I wanted exercise—to do it—
didn't want to ride a bike.

I started early in the morning, and set out. The day went
on, and I began to worry I wouldn't make it before he left.
I came to a small shopping center. I decided to call him. I
found a dime, then tried, but it wouldn't connect. A
woman in a store came out—helped me—told me how to
call (a different way I didn't know about)—seems to me
she told me the number was 6—then I called and I asked
for Richard Kenyon. She said, "Oh, you mean Dick
Kenyon." She knew him, and sounded positive—but it still
didn't connect. I couldn't get through to him. I knew he
was no longer there.

# 25 / The Path

The first year after Dick's death, Richard and I visited different churches every Sunday, looking for something—God, reasons, order, people. After a while, in some ways, we found those things outside of churches.

All my life I felt an attraction toward wanting to believe, wanted to see some order in the chaos. It always seemed to me there was something else—something, something—husband, friends, child, work, learning—but more than these—there had to be something more—something even higher.

Coming from the small town of Guthrie, from those Protestant beginnings, which I never truly felt a part of, I reached out, around, and upward, wondering—what else?

After high school I began to feel that maybe the Catholics had the answer, and I began to spend time talking to Catholic friends, wanting to understand how they believed—and if there were answers there.

Dick was Catholic, and so when we began to date I went with him to his church. Our marriage was in the Catholic church and I remember I had to go for talks with the priest, which I

231

enjoyed, because I liked discussing ideas with him, and then I had to sign a paper saying I would never lead Dick from his church, and I would raise our children in that church. I didn't like this. If I didn't sign the paper I thought there would be no marriage, and if I did I knew I wouldn't feel a total commitment inside to that promise, because who knows what is in store later in life? It was, I guess, the first clear compromise I had faced.

During the early years of our marriage we did always go to the masses, and often I liked the meditative mood, and the sense of drawing inward. When we first moved to California a year after our marriage we went to the old missions, and we both loved those—there was such a sense of all the people who had been in and around them throughout the years. I felt I could feel the imprints of all the knees that had knelt, all the feet that had walked up the adobe steps. I imagined the Indians on scaffolds painting the crude designs on the ceilings. I could almost feel the souls of the dead Indians. And I loved the bright flowers and pepper trees that often grew in the courtyards. But the ritual of the church itself began to mean less and less to Dick and to me.

We became less rigid about always attending services. We went when we felt like it, and we began to sometimes visit other churches. One Sunday in 1969, we happened to go to the large Methodist church, where we became involved with the group which eventually evolved into the gallery.

It was the beginning of the humanistic movement, the time of the encounter groups, the time of looking into ourselves, of beginning to see the "I" inside.

The seeking for spiritual answers had ended in humanness, in psychology. We all began to believe we were the answer, and our feelings were the key. *Jesus Christ, Superstar* was the closest we came to a religious experience during those years.

It was in such a limbo land, with no strong feelings, with nebulous beliefs, that we both lived the last few years we had together. Sometimes I would say to Dick, "Did I lead you astray? I guess I took you away from your church." And he would say, "Don't be silly—I would go if I wanted to."

When a woman called me, after reading my story about Johanna in *Redbook,* and said to me, "You must have a lot of faith in God," I said, "I'm not really religious, I just came to these conclusions and feelings inside."

I felt that if there was anything of God it was something inside me, inside everyone, and mostly that it was me. I wanted full credit for any of my accomplishments.

We both had been down a lot of the roads. Dick was fairly inquisitive, he probed the depths, he examined and explored the new psychology. He loved art and music. When it came to religion, I think he was not a skeptic, and neither was he a believer. Religion was just something we both felt we had evolved beyond, but now I think of course that wasn't true. We had gone beyond organized religion as we knew it, but there were and are so many truths.

I think I can safely say we were both at a kind of agnostic stage when he died, but I can also say that I don't know truly what was in his mind.

We had somehow come to the bottom of a pit. We were at a point, separate then from most friends, separate from any strong spiritual beliefs, and becoming more separate from one another. And Dick had perhaps grown separate from himself, at least separate from the Dick who wanted to live.

When Dick died the incongruity of life and death struck me. How can someone who was—just not be? It seemed incomprehensible to me. I read Raymond Moody's *Life After Life,* and I felt, and I still do feel, that the minute Dick died his spirit was set free, and that I was too—from old patterns. I felt that he could see clearly the moment after death, that if he could have seen clearly before, he wouldn't have died. In some ways, I can't believe totally that he is absolutely gone, or that anyone is.

Since that time, more and more I have a feeling of order. More and more I feel there is purpose. Things seem to fall into place, as if in a pattern. Amazing coincidences seem to happen to me. I have a feeling of trust, something I never had before. Out of disorder has come a feeling of order. Out of disharmony has come a feeling of harmony, out of purposelessness, purpose, and out of darkness has come light. There is a feeling of spirituality now—not of religion. I don't know why. I just know it is so.

I find myself on a path, looking for a source behind the art and music and words—the source behind the love I feel now permeates our every action. Seeing the world in this new way is a revelation to me, and it is too of course a new world, another world, deeper than the other one. Psychology pointed the way to the self, the god in the self, but Dick's death opened me to go beyond that, and now I seek confirmation of those feelings in certain writings, in certain people, and in myself. Now I seek the depths in a way I never did before, and I do feel that doors to perception keep opening. There is a god in the self, I believe, but now I see it is more than that. It includes the self, but goes beyond that too, includes our higher self, and connects us to nature and to others. I am beginning now to have the bare beginning of trust and faith. I can't give myself wholeheartedly to any belief, but I can say that doors are opening. There is a sense of inner guidance.

I think there are moments that are holy, and this has nothing to do with organized churches, but with maybe the source from which all those churches initially sprang. I believe we are all somehow connected. I believe there is wisdom inside we can listen to, that we need to be still and listen to.

I don't feel as if I am doing everything myself or on my own anymore, and still I don't know what to name this inner knowing.

Life is like a watercolor. I pour myself on the paper, the colors then have a life of their own—they merge and change, and I can begin to work with them, to shape and direct, carefully, but only in union with what is already occurring on that paper. When we work together, in rhythm, it is like magic. I believe now the spoken prayers will seldom be answered— they may have nothing to do with our path or pattern—but the unspoken may be, because they exist in the alertness we develop for the movement, the listening, the mating of the way the colors fall on our paper and our own action. I don't believe in asking, but in listening.

The night I prayed for Dick to come home was like crying in

a void. The scene was already set—the characters were already moving toward their destinations. I could not challenge or direct those energies already so powerfully manifesting themselves.

Accidents do exist, I believe, and maybe that is when we recklessly drive off our path or direction—stop listening—and yet even accidents ultimately seem to have their purpose and fit into a pattern, with time.

I have for years been intrigued by meditation, and a few years ago I even joined TM, but it wasn't for me—at least not then, or now. I discovered I like to meditate in several different ways, and I just do what seems comfortable to me. I like doing it at various times and in whichever way feels appropriate to me at the time. I feel then that I become clearer, calmer, in touch with myself and with my larger, higher self, which is part of everything.

I don't see this sense of "something more" as being confined in a church, in an icon or a relic. It's in the air and beyond the air. It's in our hearts and beyond. It can't be seen, held, or molded, but it can be listened to and danced with and played with, and it is ever evolving—not static.

Because I now believe in this inner guidance I now feel that when I write, it is not just me writing. I am an instrument—the vessel—the words are coming through. I'm shaping the unformed, the unspoken, giving it form, giving it words. But it comes from all around, from deep inside me, from the people in my life who through our conversations and love elaborate on the thoughts, and it comes from a stillness somewhere, far out to sea, deep inside a flower. It begins to seem that everything contributes.

We all have a path to follow, I believe—our own path—and it is constantly moving, changing. It is evolving. The idea of the path, I feel, is to not get stuck at any stage.

If Dick and I together could have come to this attitude, I wonder how different our life might have been. Pressures and roles can force us down so that we can't touch inside, and then we can't touch outside.

Whatever was inside Dick drove him to his point of departure. Whatever is inside me drives me from that point, and yet that point can't and already isn't my main reference. The point of reference is inside me. There is something, I feel, that is past passion, past violence, past learning and doing, perhaps even past love.

The paradox of coincidence has played through this whole aftermath of Dick's leaving. I don't know if these things happened before, and I just didn't notice, or if they are happening more now, as sort of signposts. And if they are, I don't know why or how, or even pretend to understand them. I just notice them.

I feel very strongly now that I meet people who are meant to be in my life, and that I know them, *recognize* them, through series of incidents I am led to them.

I feel it was not chance that led me to the job at UCSD where I came in contact with the people who filled in my life as family—not chance I came in touch with a few very special people who awakened and turned me back to life and love. It was not just chance or good luck that Dick's story was printed in *Newsweek,* and do I dare say that I found significance in the fact that the offer for this book was dated on Dick's birthday, May 8?

It is the same feeling of synchronicity I noticed with the dying of the little frog when my mother died, with the dying of the hibiscus bush when Johanna died, and with the fact that our bird died, a blue parakeet, the day after Dick died.

We seek and put symbols in our works of art because inside we know they are all around us—perhaps not coincidentally, perhaps meaningfully—as signposts to help us shape and create our own personal myths.

The boat that said "Faith" when we took the ashes to sea— the little black boy I'd never seen before who came up to me as I came out of the library feeling especially low and sad one day, who said to me, "I want to give you this pretty rose," as he handed me a beautiful pink hibiscus flower. These incidents, to me, are the hint of something more. I choose to see it that way. What further proof do I need?

We basically create our own reality. Life gives us dark clay, and asks of us to mold it into a beautiful shape. Watts Towers in Los Angeles is a perfect example of what I think one of the tasks of life is—to create from broken pieces, from little, an exquisite sculpture.

I believe now in being still and listening, not jumping to conclusions, though I still sometimes do, and in beginning to trust, though I am only just beginning to.

And I feel there is much more than I know or will ever know, and maybe that is enough to know.

In spite of chaos, in spite of enormous turmoil, or maybe because of it, I believe there is at the root of everything some sense—whether we create it, or choose to see it.

# 26 / Signs of Life—Opening the Door to Love

The opposite of death is love. We are not really alive without it. At least for me this is so.

The best sign of hope is when love trickles into our hearts and into our veins—again, and again, and once more.

Grief and shock, guilt and shame, all can cover us with a protective coating, the way a duck's feathers are oiled against penetration of water. There is love all around, only it just can't sink in.

It began to come into me slowly, and it was not a sudden change. I still stop and start—open and close—but all the time coming nearer to a feeling of wholeness.

One of the first people to touch me, to warm my heart, was Herbert Marcuse, the eighty-year-old German-Jewish philosopher, famed in the '60s because of the effect his words had on radical students. My affection for him had nothing to do with politics, or with academia, or with intellect, but had everything to do with the heart, and with life. I suppose it was because he

238

made such obvious stands for life, while Dick had made a stand, as I saw it then, for death.

I knew Marcuse simply because of my half-day job on the campus in the philosophy department. At first when I saw him in the hall, I only said hello. I wanted to talk to him, but I felt I would have to say something profound.

Then I began to notice he was a very warm, human, and teasing man. I saw also how loved he was by his coworkers, especially the graduate students and the secretaries. As in the late '60s, when he moved masses of idealistic students, his charm and appeal, in this now smaller world, hadn't faded. His twinkling blue eyes, the cigar sticking straight out of his mouth, and his hands-in-pockets walk grew to be a familiar sight to me.

One day, soon after Dick's death, I passed him in the hall. He had given me one of his books a few weeks before. I said, "I haven't read your book. I don't think my mind is right yet." He said, "I know. I know what it's like. I've lost two wives." That was all. He put the cigar back in his mouth and walked on. But those were not idle words. He knew. He had survived.

He was brilliant, thriving beneath his shock of white hair, and he was concerned with life. He was childlike, in the best sense—full of wonder and dreams. In his last book, *The Aesthetic Dimension*, (Beacon Press) he spoke of the "reconciliation of hope," and of the "affirmation of the life instincts."

He was not in an ivory tower, but was approachable and kind, and simple too, the way a Chagall painting is simple.

One gloomy day, overcome with emotion after Dick's death, and wanting to touch base with someone I admired, and who inspired me toward life, I went to his office. I told him I only wanted to let him know how much he meant to me—that he was important to me.

"Why?" he said. When I explained it was the fact he had lived so long, been through so much, and was still contributing and creating that was inspiring to me, helpful to me, he said, "Well, I hope I live for a very long time, and that you work here, and I know you as long as I live."

I made the choice to quit my job a few months later. Though

239

I had not planned it that way, my last day was also the day before Herbert and his wife left for Europe for his lecture tour.

He never returned. He died in Germany with his family and friends around. I was saddened at his death, but I felt also what a gift I had in knowing him. I still felt full of his words . . . "There is still much life for you . . . Even when one life is over, there is always more life ahead." I needed those words. His presence had drawn my attention, and his words sustained me and gave me hope.

Each person I could feel heightened by, or who gave me love, as many of my friends did, or whom I could love, seemed to me to add a lovely bead on my string of life, and to take me further from the darkest pearl.

Paul Brenner is another special person who gave me words and strength that lifted me more into sunlight and love. He is a doctor who has gone beyond traditional medicine, and who believes in love as the greatest healer. When I heard him speak at the seminar in October, 1979, his words filled my heart, as only the truth we perhaps know inside and are just waiting to hear can do. I was a parched desert, and here was rain. Two things especially moved me. He said, when asked how he felt about children who are judged defective, "I don't think those children are defective. I think the defect is in the judgment." He had put the thought so succinctly. I remembered Johanna and wished I could have felt that way initially. I knew it was true, but I also knew that few people believe that. I thought how wonderful that he could say those words and believe them. Paul's talk continued, and in a little while he said something that truly amazed me. He spoke of violence, and he said, "Even violence is an act of love"—that it is often thwarted, so restricted, that it is manifested inappropriately, but it is an attempt, and so should be honored.

This beautiful man spoke truths beyond truths. It was as if he had brought everything in my life into clearer focus. I could feel the skin all over my body quicken. I was turned around. I had never thought of Dick's act as an act of love. This was a revolutionary thought—revelationary. My whole pattern of attempting to grasp and understand what happened was altered. I remembered all the words people had said to me:

"Can't you feel his rejection of you?"

"I know it seems he didn't care about you and Richard . . ."

"He must have been a very angry man."

"He didn't love himself enough."

None of that ever seemed real. It always seemed people were trying to force thoughts on me. I know it can be argued that I was in denial, but I think those other reasons are too easy, and don't go deep enough. If love is the root of all our actions, then the worst crime we can commit against ourselves is to not express it. We have to, however we can. Dick had a lot of love to give—for people, creativity, ideas. Perhaps it was blocked. Perhaps also his final act was what he wanted most to do—regardless of what others' judgment might be.

He made a statement when he jumped, but now I feel that ultimately the message is not one of anger or despair. I used to be afraid of that message, because I didn't want to carry that torch. The message is one of love. We all have to care more, to open ourselves to love more.

Journal entry, October, 1979:
The lesson, of the act—was not for violence, but love. My task is to show love.

I thought that if Dick died for a "cause" then it had to be that it was to show how insensitive the university was, and that I needed to lash out at them—preach the horror of what happened—but I couldn't do that.

Now I see that the lesson is love. I have to show love in order to counteract the insensitivity. Even if I don't, the message they too will receive is that we have to love each other more. We have to love now.

Now it is finally clear to me. The violence will always eventually come to love if it is played out to its full extent.

If we want to prevent suicide, that is the only key. It is not in

241

books on statistics. It is not in suicide workshops. If we want to live, we have to keep learning to love, to improve the quality of our love, and to find ways to express it—music, art, teaching, writing, being with others, *really* being with others.

I think now, too, we have to own our love—"Though lovers be lost, love shall not," as Dylan Thomas has said. I can't and don't want to kill the love I've felt for Johanna, or for Dick, or for that matter, for others I've cared for deeply. So often in life we do seem to lose something just as we grasp it, but maybe that is the point. It keeps us going, and growing. If we take that love and twist it, stuff it away, try to crush it, we only crush ourselves.

Love is meant to go on—I guess even if we aren't—but every now and then, it offers us a ride.

# 27 / Learning to Love

The stillness holds its breath
Its heart begins
to beat.
A soft bird flutter,
hardly a sound.
A delicate quickening.

We begin,
like this
the unfolding—
the rose-heart
opens petals
to a silent pulse
to a stillness of breath
now held
as if it carries
the secret
of the world.

What is love? Will it fill the space left by Dick? Or is it the space left by Dick? Perhaps it is both the answer and the questions.

Rainer Maria Rilke, the poet, has said in his *Letters to a Young Poet*, ". . . the point is, to live everything, *live* the questions now. Perhaps then you will gradually, without noticing it, live along some distant day into the answer."

Once I could think of Dick's act as an act of love, the world changed for me. I now had an acceptable screen through which I could view his experience and mine. His statement was ultimately one of love, however thwarted, however painfully expressed, and so are all our life's statements—our attempts to communicate and experience love. When I realized that, I could begin the journey back to my own love.

For the first year and a half after Dick's death I sought and received some comfort and love from friends. What I experienced is something most people who have had a loss know about, I believe. It is as if you are held up by a variety of hands, which compose a sort of sea of love. There isn't one all-encompassing hug or one person to run to, to share with. This places us in a different state of consciousness and can cause us to be open to friendship in a way never before possible. It is easy to feel overwhelmed and touched by the love of friends and even strangers.

When that happens there is a kind of intimacy of sharing which is very profound. The shock and resultant surrender to fate can cause us to be pushed into a different and heightened state of awareness. And so this was the nest of love from which I could begin to grow more into my unfolding life.

When Johanna was born I had felt immediately a circle of love that existed in all our gallery friends. The impact of Dick's death was greater, and so it was at first as if silence expanded in large concentric circles—silence and isolation. With Johanna the waves rushed toward me from the beginning in love. With Dick's loss the sea drew away from me for a while, sucked the very air with it. But little by little the tide is returning, and the love is coming back, not only from others, but inside myself, and it is coming back on a higher level—a rarified level—not as big a surge, but a more exquisite and finer swell.

The waves have brought me a few very special friends,

244

women friends who are like sisters to me, and about whom I care, and a few men who are my dear and good friends.

I realized after Dick died that I had personal emotional love needs, not necessarily sexual needs, but love needs. For me the two are intertwined. I can understand love without sex, but not sex without love. But I didn't even know during that first year if I would be able to feel love. I felt my heart was frozen with guilt and pain. Now, with time, I know that is not so. I know now I can love.

People ask me, "Are you dating?" No one asks me, "Are you loving?" I have chosen to live a quiet life, have dated little, and then only old friends. And yet during this time since Dick died my heart did open to love with one man. It is not a love I can keep, or name, or enclose, and yet a love that is there. And I think it matters not who the man is, but what matters are the gifts I have received from him. One gift is that I know now I can love, and when that happens it is as if a light is turned on in the darkness. The other gift is that the feeling is now reinforced in me that love is really the fact that another is there for us. It is clearly the same lesson Dick's death taught me—that it is the spiritual connection, the meeting of souls that really matters. The physical closeness isn't necessarily the real closeness. And it is the fact that we share in another's life, and urge that other toward more life. There is a quotation I am reminded of: "To love someone is to bid him to live, and invite him to grow."

I have discovered what is necessary. It is the spiritual, almost mystical connection of love that I need. It is being in love, living in love. It is the intimacy, the sharing of a sunset, a poem, or a question, that I seek. This spiritual connection is something that, once sensed or experienced, doesn't go away.

Now I know how alive I can feel, and that love is possible. I believe now that as I am ready, things have and will come to me, that I have the love I need and want in my life right now.

If anything, life has taught me that the nature of love is that its form may run through our fingers like sand, or water, but its essence remains. The important thing is to recognize it, share it, appreciate its existence, and then—let each precious moment go. We only hold it by not holding it. It is like a river with no beginning and no end. It is moving past us, and yet is with us.

I've learned, too, it is all right to have spaces in my life. I don't have to be enveloped in love all the time. We are all, I feel, too afraid of spaces, of pauses. We become panicky if love doesn't come along when we have lost—but the truth is, love is always inside, waiting to grow, waiting to be given. It is like the words from the song, "The Rose," by Amanda McBroom: "Love, it is a flower, and you—its only seed."

I've learned, too, there are alternatives. Love has many faces. There are, in a sense, many types of lovers, and there are many kinds of love—of friends, of life, of work—and there are degrees of closeness. To have it all in one person now seems to me to be an illusion. For me love is diffused and scattered like stars, though one or two may shine brighter than others.

I feel somehow that maybe for me love will always be a mosaic—several parts can make up a whole. The only large piece in the mosaic is me—the base.

Each experience I go through now is like another bead on my string—every conversation, smile, concert, movie, book, trip I take, every person, all take me down my road to love.

And it can be for moments. Maybe those moments will be strung into nights of love, days of love, maybe even weeks, months, or years of love, but I don't expect permanence anymore with one person, and yet I hope for the permanence of loving. I have discovered I can live without a mate, even without much physical closeness, but I couldn't live without love.

I want to work not only on my ability to experience and recognize love, but most of all on my ability to give love, and to have it inside me.

Love, like a rainbow, is a gift we can be open to seeing, and it may be that we can't make it consciously appear, as much as we can just bring it into focus.

> When does it really begin,
> the love?
> When is it we can hold it in our hands,
> claim it as our own?

Ripples on water's surface
carry it
and
we watch it pass.

Our hands reach down
to feel it move gently by.

We were never meant to hold it,
love runs between our fingers,
moves on,
always heading out of vision,
always staying within vision.
When does it really end?

(July 15, 1980)

Loss has given me the realization of finiteness—that we never know "when we'll see someone again," as Richard has said. We have such little time to touch the heart of life. So I believe now in telling people when I love them, actually saying the words. For love is communication, the feeling we have touched another and they have touched us. It is the feeling we speak the same language.

If Dick and I had communicated more clearly, if he could have communicated his love, his expression, his inner drive, to the world and to me—and if we could have heard him—and if I could have clearly communicated my love, would it have helped? Would he have had to die?

There were always unspoken words. One evening at the dinner table, just weeks before he died, as I looked at him I felt I wanted to say it meant a lot to me we were together, that we'd shared so much. I was realizing it was a special kind of love—a very special experience to know someone for so long and to have shared the little and big events of our lives together. We had been through so many years together. We almost *were* each other's experiences—but I didn't say one word. Yet all of this counted for so much. I felt that perhaps the special magic of new love changes, but what we had at that point was in no way

247

less, was wonderful, real, and alive—yet I didn't say it.

There could have been joy in sharing that moment, but I didn't take the risk. I hadn't leaped from my heart to his. So I missed a chance to break through the wall he had evidently been building, and I missed a chance for a touch of oneness. What was I afraid of? That he would care? That he'd need me? That we'd get lost in each other? Joy only comes with the leap of faith, but we're afraid if we take it no one will be there to catch us. But the truth is, whether anyone is there or not, we are teaching ourselves how to fly. Are we afraid if we touch, we'll lose ourselves—we'll die? We'll die if we don't. We'll die anyway.

I know no one will ever replace Dick, for no one is ever replaced, and I wouldn't want anyone to, and I know, too, that no one will ever be everything to me. And I know that any man I meet and care about and come close to will have to understand and accept Dick's life and death too, to a degree, because if he can't, then he will be denying a big part of me. Those we've loved are always a part of us in some ways, I believe—like scattered fragments they color the mosaic of our souls. And yet, it is not all of me. I realize, too, some of this is my desire to tie all love and events in my life together, and yet I know they are inevitably connected. I believe new love is always rooted in love and experience of the past. We are never separate from it. What Dick and I shared will always be a part of me, and on another level, the qualities Dick had, of gentleness, intelligence, integrity, and caring, are still qualities I love, and respond to when I see them in someone.

Love is never new. It is somewhat recycled, grown from the roots of our past grief and love. I think, too, that especially in a situation such as mine, if my past and the acknowledgment of Dick's death are not accepted, there will always be a gap, a question. I might be loved and accepted, but then doubts could creep in. It will take a special man to love me, and I know it is only a special man I can love.

Once a strong mystical connection is felt with another, even if only once or twice in our lives, we know then in our hearts we are never truly alone. Maybe the simplest way I can say it is that I know now it is possible to meet someone who does not feel like a "stranger" to me. I trust in a sense of knowing when it

248

comes to love—a sense of rightness. New love I've felt has made a bridge from Dick's love to me and my future—between the loss of Dick and the love in me.

Love is not measured in quantity of presence, sexuality, physicalness, or time—though these elements can add and be reflections of the true closeness. The true intimacy I think is something we know in our hearts. We feel it there in relation to another. It doesn't ask for proof, and yet it contains mystery.

There is a phrase of John Fowles': "Love is the mystery between two people—not the identity."

This mystery is to be respected, for there is something almost holy about it. I guess that is why it is so difficult to talk about love. In a sense it is almost sacrilegious to try to define it—to say its name, and still the desire to understand seems intrinsic.

In some ways I think romantic love is just a very exquisite, exotic, personal, and pure form of unconditional love. Both see only perfection in the other, do not pass judgment. It is perhaps also a little like some people's view of the world when they know they are dying. They see only beauty—fall "in love" with the orange of a carrot, or the smell of a blade of grass. When in such a state, the world often says, "Oh, he/she is deluded—can't see clearly—is clouded by feelings of love," but I think the truth is those are the times we are seeing absolutely clearly. During those times our vision is *not* clouded. We see the true beauty. It is the rest of the time we are deluded—seeing the imperfection. So, for those often too brief times when we are given the gift of romantic love, we are being given a little taste or glimpse of whatever a heaven might be. It is perhaps a state of grace.

My standards for love and intimacy are deepening. In order now to feel close to someone it is important for me to feel our visions are somewhat similar. I need to feel the other person is not afraid of the depths of exploration, as well as the heights, and I need to feel something beyond pleasure. Perhaps it is joy, perhaps it is purpose. Everything has changed so drastically in my life. Now I can't help seeking more meaning. Dick's death demands something of me beyond just going on. There are more questions, if not more answers.

The perfect love for me I suppose would enclose me emotionally with another, but then would go on out past us toward some common goal or purpose or seeking—some creation. Maybe that is what children stand for after all.

When I felt an awakening to love in me I felt a true balancing of my life. I remembered the spoken prayer I had uttered with Richard that night Dick didn't come home. This spoken prayer was not answered, at least not as I wished, but when I felt love come into my life I realized that now an unspoken prayer or wish had been fulfilled. That which I asked for I didn't receive, and that which I never dreamed of asking for, I was given.

My feelings about love have changed. Now I find myself asking—How best can I love that person? And I am really asking it for the first time in my life, trying to go past my selfish needs that tried to masquerade as love.

The challenge I think is whether I can love, and not so much that I experience an equal exchange of love. I don't believe the words of the song, "You're nobody till somebody loves you," are as true as "You're nobody till you love." And I think at root is the feeling in me that maybe there is a special way to love each person—and that part of our task is to discover that way. It is as if there is a gift to be exchanged between some of us.

As love ends in grief, so grief must end in love. That is the ultimate end to the mystery and the mystical beginning, for to love means to go beyond. A different love than existed before is born, not just because one object of affection is gone, but because always we are different once we have been through such a passage.

I don't wish for happy endings, just for more beginnings, and though there are still doubts inside about my own ability and right to truly love, in my heart I know Dick would want me, more than anything, to continue loving. For whatever reasons he died, it was never so that Richard and I would not live.

Love is the fact that someone is there, and love is the fact that someone is not there. It is the space that surrounds that person we love. It is what is present when that person is with us, and it is what is left when that person is gone from us.

If the hope of unity with one person is less, the hope of unity with myself and with the world is more. And the other side of unity is expansion. Love is meant to go outward, like an ever-widening circle, from our own hearts, to another, and to the universe. Sometimes I think the purpose of love is to draw us into relation with one another, and into relation with something greater than we are.

The word "widow" means empty. And I am no longer widow, because now I feel no longer empty. I have love inside. I'm beginning to have something to give.

I don't know what's ahead. I only know my heart has been cleaved apart, and now touched and healed, it is beginning to open again.

>           *Spirit Flowers*
>     Unbidden
>     the flowers came
>
>     filled in the spaces
>     where empty cries
>     fell on God's ears.
>
>     Now
>     he hands me
>             flowers,
>             flowers,
>             flowers,
>     a wave full of flowers. . . .

>                         (5–27–80)

# Epilogue—Happily Ever After Is Now

Dick didn't die in vain. I don't believe that anyone does. Perhaps it all just comes down to being able to see the gifts. There were lessons to be learned—gifts to be taken, to be aware of, even from his death.

Some people have to endure suffering, illness, death. Others have to participate in it indirectly and deal with it, learn from it. Sometimes the afflicted person is too deep in his pain to rationally communicate his learning. He himself is a sacrifice in that sense, but there is usually another, affected by him or her, who can assimilate the learning for both and carry it on, communicate it. This too is a sacrifice. We need each other for the creation which will come from the event or experience. It is as if Dick impregnated me with his death, and I had to grow it, transform it and give it back to the world. This is my gift. And in this sense, Dick is very much a coauthor of this book.

With Dick's death I was shaken. I will never be the same. That was the gift of change. I feel that in a way my vision was lifted. I feel also I reached the point of *tabula rasa*—and I can now be imprinted as I choose.

I feel it is important to be careful with change. Maybe we have to consciously direct that point of "dangerous possibility"—not let it affect us in a negative way or in a surface way, make us bitter, angry, protective of ourselves, cause us to feel our separateness from others. Instead, if it works deeper, it can bring about a real transformation, a shaping of beauty.

Dick also gave me the gift of choice. In the awesomeness of his choice, a gift of choice was left to me. If discord, stress, separation from self and from love could lead to death, then I want to choose harmony, some peace of mind, and try to be in touch with myself and life and to begin to understand love. And yet there may have been all those elements in Dick's choice. I don't know. They certainly play through our lives in different ways. Part of my choice is to submit to the movement of life, keeping the doors open, and my heart and mind too, and beyond this, to mold and shape the events of life in such a way that the beauty and symmetry shows, in order to share.

There is a story of an Indian who made a flute of his dead love's thighbone. Maybe we have to whittle away at grief and pain in order to come to its perceivable beauty and song.

I feel, too, in some ways that the greater the negative force, the greater the potential for the positive force that can rise in response.

What can ever be said of two people? We try to touch what is real—but the images change constantly before us. Perhaps the most that can be said of lives, as they blend, touch, and dance for a while, is that dreams touch dreams sometimes.

The hopeful wife is gone—the part that thought someone could make me happy forever, or that I could make someone happy forever. There is a kind of innocence lost—but there is something else—and this new hope, born from loss, is not based on having as much as it is based on knowing and appreciating and living.

Journal entry, January 20, 1980:
Time takes off the sharp edge—that's all. I will always remember. Years from now when I'm old, I'll look at early pictures of us both and I'll see we were still tender and vulnerable. I'll see we didn't know how limited we were, and then I'll look into our eyes to try to read signs.

I'll know those little moments were everything—are every-thing. We just fail sometimes to see them shine, but the essence of life is something we hold in our hands and yet it is slipping through like bright water—water reflecting the sun and the moon and the stars—and our faces.

I used to frequently think positive events in my life were "too good to be true." Now I know nothing is really too good to be true. When those perfect, clear, happy, transitory moments happen, that's more real than anything, but hanging on, thinking they'll last forever—that's what is not real.

I don't know if there is ever anyone we lose that we don't think—I could have loved him/her better. It would be so nice to say in honesty, "No regrets."

Perhaps I did think in terms of what Dick could give me and what I wanted to give him—more than understanding or seeing what he needed. I don't even know if it would have been possible for me to give it to him, to really see his secret heart, but I wish I could have. Something he wanted and needed was never gained—a space of love no one filled enough must have pulled him away, sucked him into his own black hole, and still the scientists say black holes may be entries to other universes.

Though in some ways I feel a sense of failure—that I didn't see, wouldn't see, couldn't see, that I lived in illusion—at the same time, I feel a deep sense of hope, for Richard, for life, and for the ability of all of us humans to love.

One recent dawn, as I awakened, my eyes focused on the leaded glass butterfly Dick had made for me, hanging in a high window in my bedroom. Its luminescence was reflected on the ceiling by the rising sun. The piece itself is elegant, beautiful, finely made, at least fifty carefully cut facets, yet almost static in form. But the brilliant image, formed by the light passing through the glass, now floated above me on the white space, and was ephemeral, translucent, and appeared to be in flight—appeared released from its form.

Life is really an art work. All our lives are crystal-like, jewel-like. We only have to see it that way, and it is so.

254

Journal entry, July 30, 1980:
I walked along the late afternoon beach today. At a certain point, I decided to turn around and walk back. As I did I saw a little boy in front of me. He was in a blue rubber blow-up boat, and he looked at me directly, and he said to me, "Suicide," in a sing-songy voice, "Suicide, I'm playing suicide."

I was speechless. I just looked at him. I felt stunned. He smiled and jumped off the side again. I glanced back once, still feeling I should speak to him, but I didn't know what to say, and then I turned and I walked on, parallel to the beach, and the cool waves licked my ankles and legs, and the sun, low on the horizon, warmed my left side, and I just kept walking.

I knew Richard was out there somewhere ahead of me, riding the waves with his friend on their boards. The thought of the boy stayed with me, but the water felt lush and clean, the scent of sea air filled me, and the light shimmered on the water, like drops of liquid sun—and I just kept walking.